PENGUIN PASSNOTES

Z for Zachariah

Susan Quilliam was born in Liverpool and educated at
Liverpool University. After a period of teaching, she moved
to London where she works in publishing and as a freelance
writer. She has written a number of titles in the Passnotes
series including those on *Pride and Prejudice*, *Silas Marner*,
Romeo and Juliet, *Kes* and *Roots*.

PENGUIN PASSNOTES

ROBERT C. O'BRIEN
Z for Zachariah

SUSAN QUILLIAM
ADVISORY EDITOR: STEPHEN COOTE, M.A., PH.D.

PENGUIN BOOKS

Penguin Books Ltd, Harmondsworth, Middlesex, England
Viking Penguin Inc., 40 West 23rd Street, New York, New York 10010, U.S.A.
Penguin Books Australia Ltd, Ringwood, Victoria, Australia
Penguin Books Canada Ltd, 2801 John Street, Markham, Ontario, Canada L3R 1B4
Penguin Books (N.Z.) Ltd, 182–190 Wairau Road, Auckland 10, New Zealand

First published 1987

Interactive approach developed by Susan Quilliam

Made and printed in Great Britain by
Richard Clay Ltd, Bungay, Suffolk
Filmset in Monophoto Ehrhardt

Contents

Acknowledgements

Z for Zachariah by Robert C. O'Brien is published in the United Kingdom by Victor Gollancz Ltd, and by Fontana Lions in paperback.

The extract from *Domain* by James Herbert is reprinted by permission of New English Library Ltd.

To the Student

The purpose of this book is to help you appreciate Robert O'Brien's novel *Z for Zachariah*. It will help you to understand details of the plot. It will also help you to think about the characters, about what the writer is trying to say and how he says it. These things are most important. After all, understanding and responding to plots, characters and ideas are what make books come alive for us.

You will find this Passnote most useful after you have read *Z for Zachariah* through at least once. A first reading will reveal the plot and make you think about the lives of the people it describes and your feelings for them. Now your job will be to make those first impressions clear. You will need to read the book again and ask yourself some questions. What does the writer really mean? What do I think about this incident or that one? How does the writer make such-and-such a character come alive?

This Passnote has been designed to help you do this. It offers you background information. It also asks many questions. You may like to write answers to some of these. Others you can answer in your head. The questions are meant to make you think, feel and respond. As you answer them, you will gain a clearer knowledge of the book and of your own ideas about it. When your thoughts are indeed clear, then you will be able to write confidently because you have made yourself an alert and responsive reader.

Note: the page references are to the edition published by Fontana Lions, 1976.

Robert C. O'Brien

Robert C. O'Brien was born Robert Conly in New York City. He was educated at Columbia University and the Juillard School of Music, and worked as an editor and writer for numerous magazines and newspapers. He was a great campaigner against warfare and all forms of pollution, and *Z for Zachariah* reflects his deepest beliefs about the stupidity and tragic waste of nuclear war. He wrote a number of books for young adults, in fantasy style, which covered various topics important to him, and some of these were turned into television and cinema films. He died of cancer in 1975, leaving a wife and four children.

Summary

Z for Zachariah is written in the form of a diary. We very quickly realize what the writer's situation is. She is Ann Burden, the only survivor left in her valley after a nuclear attack has devastated the surroundings. Now she realizes that although she thought she was the only person left alive on earth, in fact someone else has survived and is coming to the valley. She is very frightened in case this person wants to harm her.

Chapter 1 begins with the entry for 20 May, where Ann explains what is happening, and thinks back to the first days after the nuclear war (pp.5–6). The entry for 21 May continues this (pp.6–8), and on 22 May, Ann finishes her story of how her family left and never came back (pp.9–10).

In Chapter 2, Ann decides to hide until she is sure the intruder is friendly, so she makes her house look uninhabited (p.11). She also tells us more about how she has survived since the war (pp.12–16). Then she retreats to a hideout, a cave in the woods.

On 24 May, she sees the intruder for the first time. It is a man, wearing a strange plastic suit and dragging a trailer (p.17). The man walks into the valley, and seems amazed and delighted that it is green and the air is pure (pp.18–19). He explores, goes into Ann's house, and finally settles there for the night (pp.20–21).

Ann still watches the stranger, unsure of how dangerous he is. And on 25 May, she watches him make a big mistake. He finds the two streams that run through the valley, and bathes in one that Ann knows to be contaminated (pp.22–6).

Chapter 4 opens, still on 25 May, with Ann describing how her family dog, missing since the war, comes back (p.27). He took food from the man, and then found Ann (pp.28–9).

On 26 May, a Sunday, Ann follows the stranger as he explores the valley (pp.30–31), finds the store (p.32), discovers the place where the deadness begins (p.33). On the way back to the house, he is violently sick (p.34).

On 27 May, at the start of Chapter 5, Ann is worried that the stranger may be seriously ill (p.35). So later that day, she walks down to the house, and finds him in his tent (pp.36–7). She brings him water and food (pp.38–9); then, realizing that there is now no point in staying in the cave, moves back down to the house again.

On the stranger's instructions, Ann tests the water of the stream for radiation, and finds the count high, which means he will be very ill and may die from the effects (pp.40–42).

The next morning, however, 29 May, the stranger, whose name is John Loomis, seems much better (p.43). He and Ann talk, she tells him her story, he explains that he came from Ithaca, walking all the way (pp.44–5). Then she invites him into the house (p.46).

Loomis tells Ann more about himself; how he was working before the war on a secret plastic which turned aside radiation (p.47). When the war came, he was working underground, and so was safe; after three months, he ventured outside wearing a suit of the plastic, which keeps him safe. he finds that no one else seemed to have survived (pp.49–51). So he kept walking south, until he found the valley.

In Chapter 7, set four days later, on 3 June, Ann describes how at first Loomis seemed better (p.52). She carried on with her farming work, and Loomis watches her (pp.53–4). In the evening, they sit together in the house (p.55), and to Loomis's delight, Ann plays the piano for him (pp.56–7). For some reason, she begins to become uneasy in his presence, and decides to sleep in the cave, but she hears that Loomis is having a nightmare and, concerned for him, stays in the house that night (pp.58–9).

The next morning, described in Chapter 8, Ann goes out to collect greens (pp.60–61), and sees a crab-apple tree in bloom. It makes her think of weddings, and she imagines happily what it would be like to marry Mr Loomis, and have children (pp.62–3).

She finds Loomis at the stream, re-testing the radiation reading (pp.64–5), and they discuss plans for the farm and the valley. Then they set off to go fishing (p.66), but Loomis begins to feel ill again, so Ann goes alone (p.67). They end the day with a festive meal (p.68).

Chapter 9 opens with Ann's description of how she gets the tractor going. She discovers how to get petrol from the nearby petrol station (pp.69–71). With it, she fills the tractor tank, and then starts ploughing (pp.72–3). She feels optimistic, but that night, Loomis becomes ill again.

Ann describes at the start of Chapter 10 how, over dinner that same evening, the radiation sickness begins again (pp.75–6). Ann cares for him as best she can (p.77), but next morning he is worse (p.78). She leaves him, to go to the brook and the store, but when she comes back Loomis has got up out of bed and is wandering round deliriously (pp.79–81). He shoots at her with his gun, but Ann stays calm and gets him back to bed (pp.82–3).

By next morning, Loomis's temperature is over 106, and he is delirious most of the time (p.84). In his delirium, he talks about what happened immediately after the war (p.85), and Ann gradually begins to understand (p.86 on) that Loomis had a colleague with him when the bomb dropped, a man named Edward (p.87). Edward wanted to use the precious suit to go out and find his family. Of course, Loomis was against this (pp.88–9), and Ann begins to suspect that he shot Edward to stop him. And when she looks at the suit, she finds bullet holes (p.90). She is horrified.

That night, Ann goes to the church to pray for Loomis's recovery. When she comes back, she sits with him, not knowing whether he will live through the night (p.91).

In Chapter 12, the diary entry for 5 June, Ann tells how she continues to look after Loomis (p.92). She feels cheered up when, on one visit to the church to pray for him, she finds a baby crow (pp.93–5). That evening, though, Loomis is no better; Ann reads him some poetry (p.95). She is still horrified at the thought he might be a murderer (pp.96–7), but tries to understand why he might have had to do it.

The next day, 6 June, she again goes to church, and also plays the piano, hoping Loomis might hear (p.98).

And in fact, as Chapter 13 opens, on 7 June, he is a little better. Ann begins to think about the future again, imagining how they could go into the outside world and get books, now they have the safe-suit (pp.99–100).

The next day, Loomis opens his eyes. Ann begins to feed him liquids, and also finds the energy to rebuild the stove, so now she can cook properly (pp.101–2).

The next diary entry is dated a week later, 15 June. Ann says it has been a happy week, ending in a celebration for her sixteenth birthday (p.103).

Each day of the week, with Ann's help, Loomis had got a little stronger. He drank some soup (p.104), fed himself (p.105), and started to concern himself with how the farm was going (pp.106 on). In fact, this led to his getting angry, when he realized that Ann had neglected the farming in order to care for him (pp.107–8). And Loomis also started to walk by himself (pp.109–10). Each day he was a little better.

Ann continues to describe this in Chapter 15, the 22 June diary entry. Loomis refuses help from Ann in his attempts to walk (p.112), and in fact starts to take charge more and more. He becomes very angry when Ann suggests she use the safe-suit (pp.113–14), and lectures her on the right way to farm (pp.114–15).

Loomis looks on (pp.116–17) as Ann works on the farm.

But she still feels uneasy. She tries to become more friendly with Loomis by talking more to him (pp.117–19), but one evening, while they talk, the conversation turns to marriage. Loomis frightens Ann badly by grabbing her hand (p.119) and in pulling away, she hits him (p.120). After that, their relationship is even more strained (pp. 121–2).

Chapter 17 is written on 30 June. A few days have passed, and Ann is now living in the cave again, upset and confused (p.123). After the hand-holding, life continues as before, but Loomis tries to be more friendly (pp.124–6). At dinner the next day, he asks Ann to read to him, though he does not seem to listen, which makes her feel uneasy (pp.126–8).

The next night, Loomis asks Ann to play the piano, and frightens her by tapping with his cane while she is playing (p.129). The night after, though, he disappears into his room after dinner, so Ann goes for a walk (pp.130–32). On the way back, she sees Loomis, and is surprised to find him walking without his cane. It disturbs her, and when she goes to bed, she simply slips her shoes off and dozes.

A while later, Ann wakes with a start to find Loomis in the room with her. He comes over to the bed, and she knows very well what he plans to do. She leaps off the bed, and when he grabs her, hits back with her elbow and runs away (pp.132–3).

Chapter 19 opens with Ann running from the house. She goes to the store and gets herself warm clothes, then climbs up to the cave where she hid before (pp.134–6). When morning comes, she watches as Faro, the dog, comes looking for her. She sends him away, and immediately realizes her mistake as Loomis ties the dog up, to use him later to track her with (p.137). Ann decides that she will not go back to the house but hopes she and Loomis can compromise and learn to live in the valley together (pp.138–9).

As she feared, Ann sees, at the start of Chapter 20, that Loomis is training Faro to track her (p.140). She decides to stay in the cave, and takes stock; she begins to build a fire (pp.141–2).

The next morning, she goes back down to the house, hoping to negotiate with Loomis. He seems unrepentant; but she offers to do the work and share the food with him, and he agrees (pp.143–4). So Ann does her day's work (pp.145–6). In the evening, she watches as Loomis drives the tractor (pp.147–8) – and regrets that he ever came to the valley.

Chapter 21 is dated several weeks later, 4 August. Much has happened to Ann in that time. For about ten days, the compromise system works but Ann still feels uneasy, and there are many things she misses (pp.148–50).

Then Loomis, who has been getting stronger all this time, begins to try to find out where Ann is hiding (p.151). And one day, needing her knife, Ann makes a big mistake, and goes back to the cave to fetch it, so giving Loomis vital information about how far away she is living (p.152). He then confiscates the tractor key (p.153), and when she goes to ask for it, tells her that he will keep things from her if she refuses to come back (pp.154–5).

Ann realizes that Loomis is working up to another attack on her (pp.156–7). And later that afternoon he drives the tractor to the store and she realizes he thinks she is living there (pp.158–62). Discovering she isn't, Loomis puts a lock on the store so Ann cannot get food (p.163).

The next morning, Ann goes down as usual to work for Loomis (p.164). As she approaches the house he shoots at her, and hits her in the ankle (p.165). Ann runs for her life, and washes her ankle in the pond; she realizes that Loomis wanted to maim her so that he could keep her prisoner in the house (pp.166–7).

Loomis chases after her in the tractor, and gets Faro to track Ann (p.168). Ann keeps ahead of them, and plans to shoot Faro so that the dog will not give her away; at the last moment, she cannot do it (p.169). Loomis finds the cave and when he leaves, and Ann goes down there, she finds all her belongings burnt (pp.169–70).

From now on, Ann lives wild. Her wound makes her feverish for several days (p.171), and sometimes she has dreams, of leaving the valley and finding children elsewhere who need her to teach them (pp.171–2). Because of this, and the disgust she feels about what has happened, Ann decides to leave the valley.

For about a month, Loomis leaves Ann alone, while she survives as best she can (pp.173–4). Then one day, she finds the door of the store open, and starts off towards it to get stocks for herself. Almost too late, she realizes it is a trap, as Loomis shoots at her again (pp.175–6). Ann runs to get her gun, and shoots back, much to Loomis's horror.

Faro has fallen into the stream, and although he finds Ann and she tries to help him, he dies the next morning (pp.177–8).

At the start of Chapter 25, 7 August, Ann is at the top of Burden Hill. She tells how she managed to steal the safe-suit (p.179).

Ann realizes after the shooting that she must take advantage of the fact that Loomis is off-guard (p.180). She packs everything and then goes to the house to leave a note for Loomis, suggesting they meet (pp.181–2).

Ann watches Loomis set off to meet her. Then she takes the wagon and drags it up the hill to the point where the 'deadness' begins. She is frightened, but calm (pp.183–4). She waits for Loomis to find her (p.185).

The final chapter of the book is written on 8 August, after Ann has said farewell to Loomis and left the valley.

Loomis arrives on the tractor, and begins to shout angrily at Ann to give him the suit back. Ann challenges him, saying she knows that he killed Edward, and he is obviously shocked by this. Ann firmly tells Loomis that she will never be his prisoner, and he begs her not to leave him. But it is too late. Ann leaves, bitterly reminding Loomis that it was she who saved his life when he was ill. As she leaves, Loomis does not try to prevent her, but instead, shows her where he saw a possible sign of more life (pp.186–8).

Ann sets off out of the valley. She walks all day, sleeps, and dreams again – of walking until she finds the children she imagined. The last words of her diary are, 'I am hopeful.'

Order of Events

Spring   Nuclear war.
            Ann Burden's family leaves
            the valley.
Oct/Nov   Last radio station dies.
Jan/Feb   John Loomis sets out to look
            for others.
Feb   Ann begins diary.
18 May   First smoke seen.
19 May   Smoke seen again.
20 May   Ann writes about smoke.   Chapter 1: entries for
                                            May 20th, 21st, 22nd

21 May   Smoke nearer.
22 May   Smoke stationary.
23 May   Ann deserts house, goes to cave.   Chapter 2:
                                                May 23rd, 24th

24 May   Ann goes to hill, sees man.
            Loomis enters valley, visits   Chapter 3:
            house, sleeps.   *May 24th, 25th*
25 May   Loomis hunts, bathes.
            Faro returns, eats with Loomis.   Chapter 4:
                                                May 25th, 26th

26 May   Loomis explores, realizes about
            creek, vomits.
27 May   Faro visits Ann; Loomis sick.   Chapter 5:
                                                May 27th, 28th

            Ann goes to Loomis, returns to
            house.
28 May   Ann tests water.
29 May   Loomis and Ann talk; Loomis   Chapter 6:
            enters house.   *May 29th*

30 May	Loomis the same; Ann works, plays piano, sleeps in house.	Chapter 7: *June 3rd*
31 May	Ann collects greens, sees crab-apple tree, attempts to fish; Loomis ill; Ann dismantles stove.	Chapter 8: *June 3rd*
1 June	Ann gets petrol, drives tractor, ploughs.	Chapter 9: *June 3rd*
2 June	Loomis ill at dinner.	Chapter 10: *June 3rd*
3 June	Loomis still ill, Ann goes to store; Loomis shoots.	
4 June	Loomis in high fever, delirious. In the afternoon, Loomis tells story of Edward; Ann checks suit. At night, Ann visits church.	Chapter 11: *June 4th*
5 June	Loomis very ill; Ann goes to church, finds crow. In the evening, she reads poem.	Chapter 12: *June 5th, 6th*
6 June	Ann at church, plays piano.	
7 June	Loomis better.	Chapter 13: *June 7th, 8th*
8 June	Loomis opens eyes; Ann erects stove.	
9 June	Loomis speaks.	Chapter 14: *June 15th*
10 June	Loomis's temperature 101.	
11 June	Loomis on solid food.	
12 June	Loomis feeds himself; Ann begins work on land.	
13 June	Loomis concerned about farming. Loomis tries to walk.	
15 June	Ann's birthday, celebration meal.	
16 June	Loomis trying to walk; Ann working on farm.	Chapter 15: *June 22nd*
17 June		

18 June		
19 June	Loomis walking; argument over books.	
20 June		
21 June		
22 June		Chapter 16: *June 24th*
23 June		
24 June	Loomis watches Ann, holds her hand.	
25 June	Loomis watches Ann work, chats, asks her to read.	Chapter 17: *June 30th*
26 June	Loomis asks Ann to play piano.	Chapter 18: *June 30th*
27 June	Ann goes for evening walk; Loomis comes to her room.	
	Ann runs away, hides in cave.	Chapter 19: *June 30th*
28 June	Loomis traps Faro.	
29 June		
30 June	Loomis tracks with Faro; Ann starts fire.	Chapter 20: *July 1st*
1 July	Ann goes to house to talk to Loomis, works; Loomis goes to store.	
2 July until approx.	Ann works for Loomis.	Chapter 21: *August 4th*
12 July	Ann slips back to cave for knife, Loomis refuses key to tractor.	
	Loomis storms the store and locks it.	Chapter 22: *August 4th*
13 July	Loomis shoots Ann, then tracks her. Ann does not shoot Faro.	Chapter 23: *August 4th*

approx. 14 July until approx. 21 July	Ann has fever, ankle heals. Has dream.	Chapter 24: *August 6th*
22 July until approx. 3 Aug.	Ann prepares to leave the valley.	
4 Aug.	Loomis lays a trap for Ann.	
5 Aug.	Faro dies. Ann sleeps in hollow tree.	
6 Aug.	Ann decides to leave the next day.	
7 Aug.	Ann sets trap for Loomis. She takes cart. Final confrontation between Ann and Loomis. Ann leaves the valley.	Chapter 25: *August 7th* Chapter 26: *August 8th*
8 Aug.	Ann sleeps overnight on the road, writes her last diary entry.	

Commentary

Chapter 1

May 20th

'I am afraid,' the book begins. 'Someone is coming.'

Do you think these are good words to begin a book? Do they immediately catch your interest? Maybe you wonder what the writer is afraid of, or who it is that is coming. Maybe you wonder who the writer is.

So as you read the beginning of *Z for Zachariah*, you may be asking yourself questions from the start. Before you read on, write down five questions you may be asking yourself. Then read the first section of the book, written on 20 May, and find out what answers you get.

Do you now know who is writing? Do you know how old, or what sex this person is? Do you know where they live, and what has happened to them? Write down what you have found out just by reading this section. In fact, we find out later that the writer is a girl called Ann Burden, and that she is nearly sixteen.

One thing you certainly know is that Ann is frightened. What is frightening her?

May 21st

The second section of Chapter 1 is written on the next day. Ann is still frightened, still wondering who is coming into the valley.

You probably noticed from the very start of the book that it was written in a diary form. Ann tells us how she began her diary, and also why. Read through the section on pp.7–8, and write down as many reasons as you can find why Ann started to write. Have you ever written a diary, or known someone who wrote one? How did that start, and what were your reasons?

Ann also tells us why she is frightened, because of what she heard over the radio before she lost contact with other people. Certainly the news she heard was very frightening – what do you think was happening out in the world that made the man on the last radio station 'plead' and cry?

Do you understand why Ann is frightened of letting someone from the outside world come into her valley?

May 22nd

Ann is still thinking through where the intruder might be and what he will be bringing with him. Notice how she works these things out logically.

She then continues her story of what happened after the war. Read through this section, pp.9–10, and then re-read the other bits in this chapter in which Ann tells us about the aftermath of the nuclear bomb. Make notes on what happened in chronological order – that is, in the order they happened to Ann.

How do you think Ann felt when her parents drove off – and then when she discovered that her brother was also missing? You can probably imagine the various stages of emotion she passed through as she gradually realized that her family was not going to come back, and that she was going to have to survive alone.

Having read the whole of this chapter, you have learnt quite a bit about the people in the book, and about the sort of things the author is trying to tell us about.

What have you learned about Ann; do you have any picture of her, or can you imagine what she looks like? What sort of person do you think she is – and do you think she has changed since she was left alone?

What have you learned about her family? There are only a few details, but you should be able to say a little about who they were and what they were like.

Although we have not met the intruder yet, he or she is already having an effect on the book. Why do you think Robert O'Brien, the author, does not immediately tell us who the intruder is and why he or she is there?

Perhaps the main thing Robert O'Brien wants to tell us about in this chapter is the effect of nuclear war. Ann has not seen or heard the direct effects of the war, not been bombed or suffered from radiation sickness – but we still realize the horror of what has happened, from the radio messages she has received, from her family's reports, from her own fears. How do you think you would have reacted if you had been in Ann's position?

Chapter 2

May 23rd

To protect herself, Ann decides to let it seem as if her house is unoccupied. Make a list of all the things she does to achieve this. What difference does she think it will make?

Then she moves up to a cave hideout she has on the hillside behind the house, and waits. She counts the hours until she sees the intruder – and that makes her think about the months going by. She is not sure of the date, but knows her birthday, 15 June, is soon.

Ann takes the time to write about how she has survived since her family left.

You may have realized that, even if you survived a nuclear war, it would not be easy to survive for very long after that. Supplies that had been stocked up before the war would soon be gone.

Write down as many things as you can think of that you would need to take care of in order to survive completely on your own. Begin with

Heat
Water

Now read Ann's account of how she coped, pp.13–16. Would you have known some of the things she knows? What sort of problems would you meet if you tried to take care of your needs after a nuclear bomb had dropped? They would be very different problems to those Ann meets.

Part of her problem is that only one of the streams in the valley is safe to use. She had a close shave when she nearly drank from the other one, but noticed just in time that it was poisoned. This fact is important later on. Can you remember why?

While telling us about how she copes, Ann also writes about her changing attitude to the intruder. She is scared, but she also wants to meet him – she wonders whether to put on new clothes to welcome him.

May 24th

In the last part of the chapter, Ann sees the intruder for the first time. It is a man, dressed in plastic and pulling a trailer. She still doesn't know whether to approach him or stay clear.

In this chapter, we learn even more about Ann. She has had to learn to cope on her own, and certainly doing this has made her grow up far more quickly than if she had still had her parents to look after her. Can you find any things that show you how much Ann has learned and changed since she was alone?

This chapter also confirms that Ann is a girl. Did you guess that? There are certainly no obvious clues. If you thought Ann was a boy, ask yourself why you thought that? How did you think a boy would react, and how did you think a girl would react, to the problems Ann faces?

For the first time, we see the intruder, through Ann's eyes. Remember that we see everything in the novel that way. He is still a strange figure, but he is coming closer, and we know a little more about him. Notice how Ann's reaction to him is changing as he gets closer.

Chapter 3

Still May 24th

Ann has watched the intruder arrive in the valley. She describes his reactions as he walks along the road, realizes that the valley is green, tests the air for radioactivity, and then joyfully takes off his helmet and breathes fresh air for the first time in many months.

Read this account carefully from p.18 to the point on p.20 when the man shouts 'Anybody here?' taking note of what Ann sees the man do. Then rewrite this incident from the stranger's point of view, including all the things Ann mentions, but told in the first person. How do you think he feels at each point?

Ann does not rush down when the man shouts out. She wants to, but she is wary. If you have read the rest of the book, decide whether you think she was right to be wary – or would it have been better if Ann had rushed to greet the stranger at this point?

After shouting, the stranger enters the house and looks round. Then, as it is getting dark, he builds a fire, eats and settles to sleep in his tent. Ann sleeps in her cave.

May 25th

The next day the man makes a mistake. Ann watches him all day, as he wakes, takes a gun and shoots a chicken, and then goes off to explore the rest of the valley.

Notice how critical Ann is of the stranger. She realizes immediately that he does not know the ways of the country – how to kill a chicken for example; in fact she knows far more than he does about how to survive. Ann also mentions that she has not fired a gun since before the war. She does however, later in the book, and not to kill an animal. Can you remember when?

The stranger sees the cows, looks at the pond, visits the church, then the store. He fires at a rabbit. He goes back to the wagon, gets soap and takes off the coverall. Then he goes for a bathe in Burden Creek.

We already know from Ann's comments in Chapter 2 that this is a big mistake, for the creek is contaminated. She is not sure what is wrong with it, but she is worried for the stranger.

Notice how, in this chapter, we see more of the stranger, watch him become familiar with the valley, learn more about him. Which of these elements about the stranger do you think are true? When you have chosen the ones you think are right, use them to write, in your own words, a paragraph about the stranger's character.

1 Happy to have found a place to stop

2 Brave to have travelled this far
3 Foolish to bathe without checking
4 Wary of people
5 Not scared of anything
6 Ready to travel on as soon as possible
7 Eager to meet people
8 Knowledgeable about country matters
9 Healthy and fit
10 Ecstatic that he has found a living valley

We also learn more about Ann. She is still frightened, but as she sees more of the stranger, she becomes more at ease with him. At first, she really wants to approach him, and then she is concerned for him. She is beginning to realize what having another person in the valley might mean.

Do you think Ann is aware of the stranger's being a man? She says he looks poetic; do you think she finds him attractive? Already, though the stranger doesn't know it, he and Ann have started to relate to each other, even if it is only at a distance.

Notice, finally, how much you have already learned about the setting of the book, the sheltered valley in America where Ann lives. Apart from occasional references to the stranger's previous life, and Ann's comments about nearby towns, all the action of the book is set in the valley. Read back over the first chapters of the book and see how much you learn about the valley. What are the landmarks? How big do you think the valley is? If you want to, draw a map of the valley; try not to make up any detail, but use only what you learn in the book. Then mark the action of the book, the trips Ann and Loomis make, on the map you have drawn, and mark each one with its correct date. This will help you form a clear plan of the movement of the book.

Chapter 4

May 25th

The first thing that Ann relates in this chapter is that the family dog, Faro, has come back. We learn that Faro used to belong to a boy who joined her family when his parents died – what do you learn about the Burden family from this?

Read the section on pp.27–9, where Ann describes Faro's return. Then choose the best answer to each of these questions.

1 Faro was
   a. a setter dog, thin and with hair missing
   b. a pointer, with all his hair missing
   c. a mongrel, mostly setter, with hair missing from his left side
   d. a mongrel, with hair missing from his left side and bones showing
2 Faro disappeared
   a. with David in the truck
   b. when he went hunting in the woods
   c. when David left
   d. because he had been tied up
3 Faro approached the stranger
   a. cautiously, but later became friendly
   b. cautiously, then later ate the food
   c. in a friendly way, though later he was cautious
   d. in a friendly way, because the man gave him food
4 When Faro found Ann in the cave
   a. she was happy to see him
   b. she was happy, but wary that he might cause trouble
   c. annoyed that he had come to the cave
   d. so shocked at his appearance that she wanted him to go away
5 Faro came to the cave
   a. because he was looking for Ann
   b. because the man had sent him there
   c. because he was looking for David
   d. because it was a place he used to play

Ann is still worried about the man finding her before she is ready.

Notice how, even at this stage, she realizes that if the man is desperate, he could end up by making her a slave.

What does happen in the end?

May 26th

This day is Sunday, when Ann usually goes to church. Today she can't, but instead follows the man as he explores the valley.

He goes to the store and gets new clothes; more and more, Ann is beginning to think of him as physically attractive.

Then he goes on further, and Ann can see him beginning to realize that there are two creeks, and that one of them is poisoned. How do you think the man feels when he realizes this?

After this, he goes to the south end of the valley, and explores the exit there. You should by now be beginning to get quite a clear idea of the geography of the valley, where things are.

On his way back to the house, the man stops and is violently sick. Ann realizes, perhaps for the first time, that something very bad is about to happen – but she is still hopeful.

In this chapter, Faro's coming back is important for a number of reasons. First, it shows Ann that it is possible to survive outside the valley, which helps her later on to decide to leave it. But mainly, Faro becomes an important part of the novel as a friend to Ann – and a danger to her.

We also learn more about both Ann and the stranger in this chapter. Read through the chapter and write down ten new things you find out about Ann, and five new things you find out about the man. Then use these, together with what you've learned in other chapters, to write about each one.

In particular, be aware that though the man does not know of Ann's existence, she thinks about him almost all the time. She has even started to wonder whether he is a suitable partner for her in the future – but also to be aware that he may try to oppress her. How is Ann changing, even over the few days we have known her?

Chapter 5

May 27th

In the morning, Faro comes to Ann to be fed, for the man is still ill. Ann is very worried about him and keeps imagining bad things. She is particularly upset because during the night she had a dream about her family returning. How do you think this makes her feel worse, more concerned for the man? She makes up her mind to go and see how he is.

May 28th

Ann is writing the diary in her own house; she has gone back. On the afternoon of the 27th, she went down to the tent and found the man, feverish and lying in his own vomit.

As Ann watches, he opens his eyes and begins talking about someone called Edward. If you have read the whole book, you will know whom the man is talking about — but Ann does not yet know.

Ann gets water for the man, and cleans him up as best she can. She says she does not know a lot about medicine, but in fact, throughout the book, she shows that she has a lot of common sense. Then she makes soup for the man.

When she takes it to him, he seems better, and for the first time they talk. You might like to imagine what each of them is thinking and feeling. In particular, each of them would have a lot of questions to ask, if only the man wasn't ill. Write down some of the questions you would want to ask if you were Ann, and some of the questions you would want to ask if you were the stranger. Which questions do they get a chance to ask at this time?

Ann now goes back to the cave and fetches some of her things. She doesn't bring back everything, which is important later on; can you remember why?

In the morning, the man is even better, and he and Ann talk quite a lot. In particular, she tells him about the poisoned stream. She tests it for radioactivity, and he explains to her what that means, and how he will get sick.

Write down what you know from the book – and from your own knowledge – about radiation sickness. Use these headings.

Causes
Symptoms
Treatment

This is the chapter where Ann and the stranger meet for the first time. Their meeting shows us a lot about them. Pick out the words from this list that describe Ann, the words that describe the stranger (some of them may be the same).

wary	friendly	hostile
grateful	confused	defensive
practical	concerned	knowledgeable
intelligent	frightened	stupid
capable	kind	surprised

If the stranger wrote a diary, how do you think he would describe their meeting? He would certainly remember less of it than Ann does, because he is feverish, but he also has strong feelings about it. Write two or three paragraphs as if you were the stranger, describing what happens and how he feels.

Up to this point, we have heard very little about the actual horrors of nuclear war. Now the reality of it is about to hit the valley. How do you think the stranger, and Ann, feel about this? Their experiences of nuclear war are so far very different, but now they will have to work together.

Chapter 6

May 29th

The next day, feeling cheerful, Ann takes the man his breakfast. She finds out that his name is John Loomis; she calls him Mr Loomis throughout the book. What does this show you about their relationship?

Over breakfast Loomis and Ann have their first real conversation in the book. What they say to each other in some ways shows us how their relationship will develop. Complete these sentences to explain what you learn about their relationship.

1 Ann's first words to Loomis show us ...
2 Loomis's reaction to the food shows us ...
3 Loomis's asking whether Ann is by herself makes Ann feel ...
4 Loomis is amazed that Ann has managed alone; this shows us ...
5 Ann takes it for granted that she has managed alone; this shows us ...
6 Loomis understands why the valley has escaped, which tells us ...
7 Loomis's reaction to Ann's description of her family disappearing shows us ...
8 Ann's offering to let Loomis stay in the house shows us ...
9 Loomis's saying 'the house is yours' shows us ...
10 Ann's saying 'You can lean on me' shows us ...

Once in the house, Loomis sleeps, and Ann works until lunch-time. Then they talk again, and Loomis tells Ann his story. It is the only occasion in the book where we really get to hear about the outside world.

Read Loomis's story for yourself, on pp.46–51. Then write about a paragraph summarizing Loomis's story from when he was working as a graduate student to when he arrived at the valley. Write it in the first person, as if Loomis was telling it, and include all the main facts.

Be particularly aware of what Loomis tells Ann, and what he doesn't tell her.

When Loomis has finished, Ann herself realizes that he has not mentioned everything. She queries the name Edward, which he muttered when delirious – but Loomis just says Edward was a colleague. It's obvious though that he is disturbed by the name; how does Ann know this?

In this chapter, you should be gaining a much clearer idea of what Loomis is like. Do you, at this point in the book, like him? If so, mention a few things that you like about him, and if not, mention a few things that make you feel negative.

Do you think Ann likes Loomis? She is certainly happy to have someone else to talk to. Does she feel totally positive about him? How do you think the author wants us to see their relationship at this point – are we meant to feel good about Loomis, or always feel suspicious of him?

How do you think Loomis feels about Ann? Does he see her as a child, or as a woman? Does he consider her to be his equal?

This chapter gives us the clearest idea so far of what has happened outside the valley. It is one of the few references to Loomis's previous life in any detail, or to life outside, until Ann decides to leave. Why do you think the author doesn't tell us more about the outside world, or about the horrors of nuclear war?

Chapter 7

June 3rd

Ann writes, four days later, about what has happened in the time between.

On the first day, Loomis seems the same; Ann leaves him, to do her essential work around the farm. She goes to the store and digs the garden, with Faro the dog for company. She seems to know exactly what she is doing, and to have planned carefully how she will manage for food. What does this show you about Ann?

While she is digging, Loomis comes to watch her. He suggests she use the tractor to save energy, and Ann has to admit she knows very little about electricity. Read the whole of this conversation, on p.54, and then decide which of these statements is nearest the truth.

1 Loomis hates women.
2 Loomis has no real idea of what Ann is capable of.
3 Ann accepts Loomis as having more knowledge than she has.
4 Ann considers she is incapable of learning about certain things.
5 Ann is more intelligent than either of them think she is.
6 Loomis tends to categorize women as being less strong than men.

Write a few sentences about what you've learned so far about how each of them imagines men and women are, and how men and women should behave.

After the work is done, Ann and Loomis walk back to the house. On the way, they watch a sunset, and Loomis puts his hand on Ann's shoulder. She imagines he needs support, and feels proud to help him. Do you think her assessment of the situation is correct?

After dinner, Ann gets worried that there is nothing for Loomis to do; she offers to play the piano, and he eagerly says yes. After she has finished playing, Loomis comments 'This is the best evening I've ever spent' – and angrily repeats 'ever'. What do you think his thoughts and feelings are at that time; why do you think he gets angry?

At any rate, his anger disturbs Ann. Do you believe she has any idea how Loomis is feeling at this time? Her reaction is to want to retreat to safety, and she is on her way to the cave when she realizes that Loomis is delirious again. She hears him having a nightmare, again about Edward. So Ann decides to stay in the house for the night in case she is needed. What does this decision show you about her?

The title of the book, *Z for Zachariah*, seems a strange one. In this chapter, Ann explains that the last letter in her alphabet book was 'Z for Zachariah'; like Loomis, the last man. Do you think, as Ann does, that Loomis is the last man left alive? Does Ann change her mind later in the book?

In this chapter, it is as if the threat of the war, the threat of Loomis getting ill, had retreated for a while. We have a chapter of peace and calm, of Ann and Loomis getting to know one another, and developing their relationship. What more do you learn about them in this chapter?

In particular, who do you think has the power in the relationship? Certainly Ann is physically strong, while Loomis is, at the moment, weak. But he is already trying to take charge, and to organize her. How is Ann reacting to this? She is still wary of him, and learning very quickly what she can and cannot do.

Chapter 8

Ann continues her account of what has happened over the last three days.

She wakes up early, and goes to collect wild greens, partly because she wants to eat some, partly for Loomis. She is happy, particularly when Loomis seems better.

Ann walks across the fields, with Faro, and sees a rabbit. She picks the greens – and is about to go back home when she smells, and then sees, a crab-apple tree in bloom. Ann describes the tree, which seems to her incredibly beautiful. If you don't know what a crab-apple tree looks like, you might want to find a picture of one, so that you know what Ann was seeing.

It is, however, what Ann thinks of when she sees the tree that is important. She thinks of getting married. She says that she has only been on one date with a boy, though there were boys in her class at school. This means that she has had very little experience in relationships; she has no real idea of what marriage involves.

Think about each of these questions.

What does Ann know about relationships between men and women? Who did she know who had such relationships?

What does Ann know about family life, and the problems of bringing up a family? What will she have learnt from her family?

Does Ann know about sexuality? How might she know these things? What difference will living on a farm have made?

What is Ann's idea of married life; is she more concerned with the wedding ceremony or what life will be like after she is married? How much has she thought about what marriage to Loomis would be like?

Now write about Ann's ideas on love and marriage at this point in the book. She says that Loomis has not indicated 'the slightest interest' in any such idea. Is she right, do you think?

Going back home, Ann finds that Loomis has got up; immediately worried, she finds him down at the stream, re-testing the water for radioactivity. He has also thought about using the water as power. Ann and he talk about this, and about finding an electric motor to use the power.

After breakfast, when Ann sets off to fish, Loomis says he wants to come with her. He doesn't know how to fish, but Ann says she will show him, another example of how, while Loomis is very knowledgeable, Ann has knowledge he doesn't have.

On the way, however, Loomis becomes ill, and Ann takes him home and then fishes alone. This is the first sign that the sickness is about to come back, and it worries them both.

After fishing, while Loomis sleeps, Ann goes to the barn and begins to take the stove apart in preparation for bringing it to the kitchen. She manages well, even though it is heavy. Despite the fact that she thinks she knows nothing about such things, Ann can certainly learn.

This chapter, another lull before the storm of Loomis's renewed illness, also starts us thinking about the future Ann and Loomis might have together. You should have enough information by now to decide for yourself whether you like each of them. But do you think that they could make a good relationship, a good marriage, together?

Remember that in some ways, the strong feelings that we call romance may not be as important to Ann and Loomis as they might be to us. They may each have other reasons for wanting to have a relationship. What might these reasons be?

Thinking of marriage is certainly a sign that Ann is growing up, changing the way she reacts to things. But her idea of marriage is still very unclear.

In another way, too, Ann is developing. She is beginning to get more confidence in her ability to do things, even things that she may not have thought were woman's work.

Chapter 9

Ann is still describing the events of the last three days.

The next morning, she finds Loomis reading in bed; he has found out how to work the pump on the petrol store, without needing to use electricity. He explains to Ann, shows her which handle to turn, and she goes down to the store.

Once there, she follows the instructions, and eventually begins to pump. She smells petrol, fills a container, and carries it to the barn to fill the tractor tank. She remembers how to start the tractor by hand, and in a few moments has it working. She proudly drives the tractor across to the house, rather expecting Loomis to be delighted.

But he is 'surprisingly matter-of-fact' about it all; how do you think Ann feels about his reaction?

After starting the tractor, Ann immediately hitches on the plough. She has decided to plough a small field to plant sweetcorn, beans and peas. She realizes now, only too well, that she really needs to be growing things to enable her to survive when the food from the store runs out, as it will. Ann has thought carefully about how to tackle this problem, what to plant and how to do so. Now, with the tractor, her job will be easy.

As she is ploughing, Ann feels really happy; she remembers a poem which she likes, and thinks of herself, like the person in the poem, as being a scribe (someone who keeps an account of what is happening) for the earth. She also feels very optimistic about the future, now that Loomis is there.

This is probably the point in the book at which Ann is happiest; she has company, she has got the tractor going, she feels she is going to survive, and she has no idea of the horrors that lie in store for her.

But that night, Loomis's temperature rises, and the sickness comes again.

Reading this chapter, the last of the peaceful chapters before Loomis becomes ill, it seems as if everything is going well. Loomis and Ann are beginning to work together, and his arrival in the valley has certainly made a change for the better.

How do you think Ann has changed, just since Loomis has arrived? How have her ideas of the future changed?

But all is not so well. Already we see that Ann cannot expect the sort of emotional reaction from Loomis that she would like. She is happy when she is alone, and when she can dream of a future the way she plans it – but the reality of coexisting with another person may be very different.

Also, we begin to realize that, although the war has not touched the valley itself, it has affected it. For the first time, Ann comes face to face with the realization that she is not safe. If she cannot grow enough food, she will not survive.

All these things prepare the way for the terrible events which follow.

Chapter 10

June 3rd (*continued*)

Ann tells how, the previous evening, Loomis did not want to eat dinner, felt cold, and retreated to his bedroom. Both of them realize that this is the beginning of the illness, and both are frightened.

However Ann seems to cope better than Loomis does, 'as if when he got weaker, I got stronger'. She plans how to take care of him, and, using all her common sense, carries it through.

Read through this chapter, and the following ones up to the point where Loomis starts to get better, on or about p.103. Write notes as you go on just how Ann takes care of Loomis, and helps his recovery. She actually does a lot of things, and behaves very sensibly, even though we know that she feels inadequate.

After Ann puts Loomis to bed and gets him warm, he turns to her and says 'Poor Ann Burden ... You're going to wish I had never come.' What does he mean by this? Is he in fact right that Ann will wish he'd never come?

In turn, Ann apologizes for not warning Loomis about the stream, but he takes responsibility for this himself, and this shows us something about his character.

In the morning, Ann carries on with her work as usual, but when she comes back to the house, Loomis has got out of bed and chilled himself.

Later that day, she again has to go out, this time to the store, tells him she is going, and is back very soon. But Loomis, thinking he has heard someone in the house (Who does he probably imagine he hears?) is once more out of bed, and shooting with the gun.

Ann realizes that he cannot be left alone, and so decides to stay with him from then on. This causes trouble later – can you remember why?

This chapter marks the start of Loomis's illness – and also really the end of any possibility of their having a relationship. For from this point on, Loomis changes, and Ann's attitude towards him changes too.

Choose three of these statements and write about them, showing how they add to the breakdown in Ann and Loomis's relationship.

1 Ann feels guilty that she let Loomis bathe in the creek.
2 Loomis blames Ann for going to milk the cow.
3 Loomis reassures Ann that he will be all right when she goes to the store, and is not all right.
4 Loomis shoots at Ann's house.
5 Ann begins to suspect Loomis is hiding something from her.

Despite all these things, Ann cares for Loomis more and more. Also, she becomes more and more able to handle difficult situations, such as caring for someone who is delirious, coping when someone is pointing a gun at her.

Have you ever cared for someone who is ill? How did you cope? Did you find you didn't know what to do – and did you then learn what to do? Did you find you were coping better than you thought you would? How do you think you would have handled Ann's situation in having to look after Loomis?

Chapter 11

June 4th

Loomis's temperature gets higher and higher, and he is delirious most of the time. Ann cares for him still, bringing him food and keeping him warm. But there is very little she can do.

Also, through the delirium, Ann is learning more about Loomis's story, and what she finds out horrifies her. He continues to think he sees Edward, even though Ann reassures him. Then he worries about where the safe-suit is, until in the end, she places it where he can see it.

Although Ann tries to help, in fact Loomis cannot be reassured, for not only is he delirious, but he is also remembering something that troubles him. He is so out of contact with reality that nothing Ann does can reach him.

He slips into what Ann calls 'another nightmare'. She doesn't realize yet that it is the truth, not a dream. Loomis talks to Edward, hearing Edward's replies in his head. Ann pieces the story together, bit by bit.

Put these sentences in order, to put together, bit by bit, Loomis's story.

1 Edward wanted to go out and find his family.
2 At first they were afraid to go out.
3 He wanted to use the safe-suit to go outside.
4 Edward and Loomis were colleagues.
5 There was a terrible argument.
6 Loomis refused.
7 Loomis told Edward that no one would have survived.
8 Loomis shot Edward.
9 Edward pleaded with Loomis.
10 They were together, underground, when the bombing began.
11 Edward tried to take the safe-suit by force.
12 Edward said he would bring the suit back, but Loomis did not believe him.

When Ann hears this story, she is appalled. At first, she cannot believe what she is hearing. She goes to the safe-suit and checks it. Sure enough, she finds bullet holes, and realizes that Edward must have been killed when Loomis shot him.

Of course, realizing this must have a big effect on Ann. It is not until the next chapter that she writes about it in detail, but you can probably imagine what she is thinking and feeling when she realizes what Loomis has done. Think about this carefully, then write a few paragraphs, as if you were Ann, which might be an additional diary entry for 4 June. Say how you are feeling, what your thoughts are, how your attitude to Loomis has changed since you realized what has happened.

In fact, a little while later, realizing that Loomis is so weak that he could not harm himself if she left, Ann goes down to the church to pray for him. 'Even though he may be a murderer, I do not want him to die' (p.91).

You may have noticed that Ann does turn to religion. It is probably that her family was religious; certainly for a valley to have only two farms but still have a church suggests that she and her family went to church regularly. You may or may not believe in religion (Loomis doesn't, and later in the book this leads to arguments), but try to realize how it helps Ann when she has problems. Read this list of possible reasons why she goes to the church, and when you have chosen the one or ones that seem nearest the truth, use them to write a paragraph on Ann's reasons for going to church.

1 Ann doesn't believe in God.
2 Ann believes in God and thinks he can help.
3 Ann feels better and stronger after she has been to church.
4 Ann finds the church a peaceful place to be.
5 Ann thinks Loomis would want her to go to church and pray for him.
6 Ann likes to go to church and see the baby birds.
7 Ann does not know what else to do other than go to the church.
8 Ann realizes that there is nothing else she can do to help Loomis, and hopes praying might help.

Chapter 12

June 5th

Loomis lives through the night, though at one point Ann thinks his breathing has stopped. In the morning, she goes to church again with Faro, to pray and to think.

When she reaches the church, Faro 'comes to a point' (p.93), indicating something unusual, and Ann sees that there is a baby crow on the church floor. It has obviously fallen out of one of the crow's nests built in the church steeple.

Ann takes the bird outside, where its parents can find it, and feels particularly hopeful after this. She explains that when she was young, she thought that birds were prayers, flying up to heaven on their wings.

Why do you think the author includes this incident where Ann finds the bird? What does the way she reacts show us about her personality? And is the bird, in fact, a signal that something good is going to happen? What other reasons might the author have for writing about this episode?

Back at the house, Ann finds Loomis no better. She reads to him, from a book of poetry she likes. If you turn to p.96 in this book, you will find the poem she reads. Why do you think Ann likes that particular poem? Do you think it was a good choice to read to Loomis at that time? Did it help Ann?

After reading, Ann sits and thinks over what she has found out about Loomis. She does not want to believe that the man she hoped to marry is a murderer, but has to accept that it might be so. Read over the section on pp.96–7, where Ann thinks this problem through, and answer these questions.

1 Ann thinks that Loomis's action might have been self-defence because
    a. Edward attacked Loomis with a gun
    b. Loomis attacked Edward with a gun
    c. Edward's taking the suit might have meant Loomis died
    d. Edward's taking the suit might have meant that both of them died
2 Ann think Loomis might have been justified in keeping the suit for all these reasons *except*
    a. it might help communication between people who were left
    b. he might be thinking of human survival
    c. he thought of it as the only useful thing left
    d. he was concerned about his work being recognized and not wasted
3 Ann thinks Loomis should have let Edward borrow the suit if
    a. he was sure of getting it back
    b. Edward really meant to return the suit
    c. Loomis trusted Edward
    d. he didn't want it for himself
4 Ann's final conclusion on the matter is that
    a. she needs to ask Loomis what Edward was like
    b. she needs to find out what Loomis is like
    c. she must wait to see if Loomis discovers civilization
    d. she needs to keep all this a secret from Loomis

Consider Ann's attitude to the whole thing. Do you think she is acting maturely, thinking it through, or is she panicking? Does all this change her, help her to grow up?

Think about your own attitude to what Loomis did. Do you think he is to blame for what happened? Do you think he should have done something different?

Take a piece of paper. On the left, write down as many reasons as you can think of why Loomis may have been wrong in what he did. On the right, put down as many reasons as you can think of why this action may have been right. Do you have any difficulties in thinking of reasons for one side or another? Discuss the problem with someone else who knows the book. What do they think? Do your opinions change? Write a paragraph on what your opinions are.

How do you think you would react in Loomis's position? Would you kill Edward? Would you let him take the suit? What would you need to know before you made your decision?

How do you think that this whole experience has changed Loomis? How do you think it would have changed you if you had been in his position?

June 6th

In the morning, Loomis seems no better. Ann goes to church, prays, and takes flowers back with her for his bedside. She feels that 'if I did [give up], he would too' (p.97). Notice how the crisis in Loomis's illness comes at the same time as the crisis in the way Ann relates to him. Robert O'Brien builds up the tension so that, as we are worrying about whether Loomis will live, we are also horrified at the thought that he might be a murderer.

When Ann gets back to the house, Loomis's high breathing rate has fallen, and he seems a little better. She plays the piano to him, hoping he will hear it.

This small section is the turning-point of Loomis's illness. From this point, he does indeed get better.

It is also the turning-point for Ann and Loomis's relationship. After this, knowing what she knows, Ann never trusts him again, though she is prepared to. It is possible too, that Loomis is changed by the illness.

Chapter 13

June 7th

Loomis seems better, so Ann changes his sheets and clothes, which is not a pleasant job.

Her thoughts turn to the fact that she has to realize that her plans of a few years ago, to be a teacher, will never be fulfilled. She likes books and reading; they have always been very important to her, and she had always planned to be an English teacher.

Now none of that will happen. She has to resign herself to staying in the valley, and making the most of life there. (Or does she?) But to bring more interest into her life, she wonders if she could bring more books from nearby Ogdentown, now that Loomis is here with the safe-suit.

 Notice how Ann, having shared her home, her food, everything she has with Loomis, expects he will share what he has with her. Is she right?

June 8th

Loomis opens his eyes and, though he is very weak, drinks water and some custard that Ann makes.

In the meantime, Ann decides to bring the stove to the house. Now she has the tractor, she can carry it. She dismantles it, transports it, and puts it together again alone, working out what she should do on each step of the way. She is very proud of herself.

This chapter marks the consolidation of Loomis's recovery. From now on, he gets stronger and stronger, and as he does the battle between him and Ann increases. But for the moment, she is still in control.

Notice how, as she worries less about Loomis, Ann's thoughts turn more to the outside world, getting the stove into the house, getting books from outside the valley. She easily tackles those jobs that Loomis probably thinks she couldn't do, such as transporting the stove, jobs which are not often seen as women's jobs. She has much more confidence in herself than before.

Chapter 14

June 15th

Ann is writing a week later, on her birthday. She describes how amazed Loomis was when she prepared a birthday meal, with candles, silver and china. He described it as a miracle; Ann says that the miracle is his recovery.

Notice how important Ann's birthday is to her. She was concerned about getting the date correct at the very beginning of the book, and has looked forward to the celebration for a while.

She describes the week. After the first improvement, Loomis wakes up the next day, and speaks to Ann, conscious and aware of what is happening. He describes the illness as he experienced it, particularly the parts when he seemed to be 'floating away', hovering on the edge of death. It was Ann's playing that brought him back.

Notice that even now, when Loomis is first recovering, he does not thank Ann, or seem to realize that she has saved his life. Do you think he realizes?

Each day, he is a little better, eating more solid food, and eventually feeding himself. It seems important to him to be as independent as he can be as soon as possible; does this show you anything about him?

In the meantime, Ann has turned her attention to the farming. It is urgent that she gets the work underway as soon as possible, otherwise there will be no food. Throughout the book, in fact, there is always this sense of steady effort, which cannot stop, to work towards the production of food. Otherwise, they will not survive.

And it is this fear that makes Loomis angry with Ann when he realizes that during his illness she did not tend the farm. He is particularly cross, as religion is not important to him, that she spent some time in church.

Even though Loomis is frightened, however, it is difficult to sympathize with him in the way he speaks to Ann about this.

Read the section on pp.107–8 where their conversation takes place. Then pick out the word that Loomis speaks that shows us he is critical of Ann. Also, pick out the words that the author uses that describe the way in which Loomis speaks, the tone of his voice.

What do you learn by picking out these words?

What points is Loomis trying to make in this conversation? List three of them. Is he right to tell Ann these things? How could Loomis have expressed his thoughts and feelings about all this to Ann without making her feel it was a 'scolding'? What words, what tones of voice could he have used? Rewrite this scene, so that Loomis makes all the points he wants to make, yet still remains friends with Ann.

As a result of this talk, Ann does indeed start the planting, but she begins to realize that living with Loomis is not going to be easy. 'He considered the valley as much his as mine. I would have to get used to the idea' (p.108). Is Loomis right to do this?

Wanting to be independent yet again, Loomis tries to walk – and he insists on doing this all by himself. This shows us a lot about him, and is in fact one of the parts of his character that leads to trouble later on.

In this chapter, we see that Loomis does not consider Ann to be capable of very much. Also, he regards the valley as as much his as hers. Ann is wary, but still concerned, and willing to share what she has because in the long run it may be the only way. And, despite the problems she has with Loomis, Ann regards this week as happy, for she has company and the future seems hopeful. To some extent, she has been able to forget what she learned about Loomis when he was ill.

However we can already see Ann and Loomis starting their struggle for power, man against woman, older against younger.

Chapter 15

June 22nd

Ann is again writing her diary after a week's break, covering the whole week in one diary entry.

She first writes about Loomis's efforts to walk. Although she tries to give him support and encouragement, he refuses it. It may be because he cannot accept support for himself that he seems so unable to give Ann any.

In fact, their second disagreement takes place fairly soon, when

Ann mentions the possibility of getting books from Ogdentown. Loomis is willing to discuss the matter when it is about books he regards as useful, but as soon as Ann asks about books she wants, he dismisses the idea. He does not seem to realize that her needs, though not as practical as his, are nevertheless important.

And when Ann suggests that she use the safe-suit, as Loomis is not yet well, he becomes extremely angry. There could be many reasons for this. Ann suggests one or two; how many others can you think of? Do you sympathize with Loomis for wanting to keep control of the suit, or do you think he is wrong?

When the conversation continues, Loomis again overrules Ann, about what they should plant. Again, Ann sees that he is right in some ways, but nevertheless, she feels hurt. How do you think Ann feels throughout this chapter, as her disagreements with Loomis get more serious, and the two of them struggle for control? Complete these sentences.

1 When Loomis walks for the first time, Ann feels . . .
2 Loomis's wanting to walk alone makes Ann feel . . .
3 When Loomis seems to be agreeing to go to Ogdentown, Ann feels . . .
4 When he was not interested in bringing back Shakespeare books, Ann feels . . .
5 When Loomis tells Ann off for offering to wear the safe-suit, she feels . . .
6 Whem Loomis contradicts Ann over the planting, she feels . . .
7 When Loomis talks of starting a colony, Ann feels . . .

Have you ever been in a situation where you have been overruled, perhaps by someone older than you? Has there been a time when you have felt your needs have not been listened to, or taken account of? What about a time when you've known you know best, but someone else hasn't realized this. How have you reacted? Has the situation changed, and have you then been listened to?

You are probably getting some idea by now of the various emotions both Ann and Loomis are feeling in this period after the illness. You might like to think of how, if both of them had acted differently, things might have been different between them.

Chapter 16

June 24th

Ann continues planting, under Loomis's orders. Even though the farming is going well, she feels uneasy at what is happening between her and Loomis.

He has begun to feel well enough to sit out on the porch, watching Ann as she works. She dresses him warmly in some of her father's clothes and, on 23 June, he sits on the back porch all morning and part of the afternoon.

In the evening, Ann puts the dinner on to cook, and then goes to sit with Loomis on the porch to keep him company. She wants to make an effort to get to know him, for all she really knows about him is what she has heard when he was delirious. She reckons that he does not talk about the past because of the bad memories he has.

So Ann asks about Loomis's childhood, when he was young, when he was at college, and in the Navy. Then, she asks if he was ever married.

To Ann, this is an innocent question – she sees Loomis's being married (or not), as just one of those things that make up his past history. To Loomis, the question is far more important. Why is this? What do you think Loomis himself thinks when Ann asks that question?

His reaction is immediate and strong. He reaches over and takes Ann's hand. She is startled and uneasy as he queries why she asked that question. There is no gentleness as he holds her hand, even when she tries to pull away. Instead, he tightens his grip, Ann falls towards him, and as she does so, her hand hits him in the face.

Loomis is angry and shocked. Ann escapes to the kitchen, shaken and frightened. She thinks back to boys she has known in the past, to the other time she held Loomis's hand, when he was ill. She realizes how different this all is. Read Ann's comments on pp.121–2; what are the differences between the previous times she has been close to a man and this one?

In fact, this is the first time that we (and Ann) realize that the fact that Loomis is a man, and Ann a woman, may be a problem. When he first arrived, Ann dreamed of a romantic spring wedding. Loomis does not feel romantic towards Ann, but he certainly is attracted to her physically. For her, it would have been an equal partnership, a marriage. Loomis is more concerned with having control over her, even in this.

What do you think Loomis is thinking at this point? Is he trying to take control? Is he perhaps scared or shy of Ann, or just not used to women? What do you think he feels when she hits him? It certainly changes what happens between them, even though Ann did not intend it to happen.

The incident makes Ann aware of the very real danger of living with Loomis. In this chapter, as in many of the others, she grows up suddenly, realizing her own power as a woman, and yet also realizing that, almost because of that power, she may need to defend herself if she is to survive.

Chapter 17

June 30th

Ann is writing some days later. She is living in the cave again, and is telling the story of what has happened in the intervening time.

The morning after the 'hand-holding', Ann gathers the eggs, and takes Loomis his breakfast. She still feels tense, and their conversation, about fertilizers, is strained. Then, when she is driving the tractor, she notices Loomis on the porch, watching her, and that makes her feel nervous.

In the evening, for the first time, Loomis comes into the dining-room to eat, saying he is now well enough to eat sitting up. He tries to create small talk, and after dinner, even asks Ann to read aloud to him. She is not eager, but does so, and becomes even more worried when she realizes, half-way through, that Loomis is not even listening to her. She feels he has played a trick on her, and is angry, but tells herself that if it is what he wants, and will help him to recover, then she is willing to help.

The fact that Ann tells us at the beginning of this chapter that she is back in the cave, shows us that something very bad has happened.

Because of this, her account of what happens becomes doubly frightening. When the makers of horror films show the heroine heading towards a terror that we know is going to happen, but she is unaware of, they use the same technique.

What game is Loomis playing at this point? What are his reasons for acting as he does over these few chapters? Complete these sentences with your own thoughts about the motivation of the characters.

Loomis watches Ann from the porch because ...
He comes to eat in the dining-room in order to ...
He makes small talk with her because ...
He asks Ann to read to him so that ...
He does not really listen to her reading because ...
Ann is uneasy at Loomis's watching her because ...
She feels unhappy at his increased mobility because ...
She continues to read to him so that ...

Chapter 18

Still June 30th

The following evening, Loomis asks Ann to play the piano. Look back at your suggestions as to his motivation, and see if you can tell why he does this – what tactics is he using?

Ann plays, but is scared in case he creeps up behind her. Then she hears Loomis's cane tapping behind her. When she turns round suddenly, he is sitting innocently listening to her. What does she guess he is doing? What does he want her to feel?

After this, Ann cannot play any longer, and goes to bed, frightened and worried. It is as if Loomis is playing a game of cat and mouse with her. She even worries that he is getting better – for that will mean he will be able to control what is happening more.

The following night, Loomis does not ask Ann to read or play. She goes out for a walk with Faro, and sits on the church steps for a while. On her way back to the house, to her surprise she sees Loomis walking to the wagon. She is amazed to see that he is not using his cane, and realizes immediately that he has lied to her about how strong he is. He checks the safe-suit, then heads back to the house. Even more worried, Ann thinks for a while, and when she goes back inside, lies down on the bed with her clothes still on and falls asleep.

She is woken by the sound of Faro growling, and she realizes that Loomis is in the room with her. At first she tries to lie quietly, hoping he will go away, but he comes over to the bed and begins touching her. She knows at once that he is going to rape her, and as he moves to pin her to the bed, she makes a leap for the door.

Loomis grabs Ann's ankle, pulling her back on to the bed, then he grips her shirt. She lunges forward, hears her shirt rip under his fingers, and hits back with her elbow, winding him. She runs out of the door and away to safety.

This, the second climax of the book (what are the others?), finally breaks any links there have been between Ann and Loomis. All is out in the open – they are enemies.

First, Loomis plays cat and mouse games with Ann, then he attempts to rape her. His reasons for doing this are never made quite clear, because the author never speaks through Loomis's mind, and Ann can only guess what he is thinking. He certainly desires Ann, but equally certainly the attempted rape is a way of proving his power over her, and establishing that he is in control. In fact, Ann escapes. What does this show us about her, her character and what the author is saying about the power Loomis has? What is the author saying, too, about the relationship between men and women?

Why does the author include the attempted rape in the book? Would it have been enough just to have Loomis make a pass at Ann – or just to steal her farm and drive her out? Would it have been better to have Loomis succeed in the rape attempt?

Do you find anything at all in Loomis that makes you sympathize with him? Imagine you are Loomis after Ann has run out of the house. Write five sentences, each beginning with the words 'I feel . . .', then use them to write a paragraph about Loomis's feelings. What do you think he does once Ann has left?

Chapter 19

June 30th (*continued*)

Once out of the house, Ann runs as fast as she can, eventually coming to a stop behind the store. Loomis does not seem to be following. At first she hardly thinks – she seems to be in shock. Then she realizes how cold she is, so she gets new clothes from the store.

In the store, Ann gets very scared when the door blows shut in the wind, but she manages to get more clothes, shoes and a candle. She then drinks some water from the brook, and goes up to the cave. She spends the rest of the night watching the house.

First of all, Faro comes, picking up Ann's trail. Loomis follows him, trying to find Ann. Faro eventually tracks Ann to the cave, but she has taken such a long way round that Loomis cannot follow him. However, when Faro returns to the house, Loomis feeds him; then, while Faro is concentrating on the meat, he ties Faro up.

Faro struggles and struggles, but cannot escape.

Ann begins to think of the practicalities of the situation. She must keep working on the farm, or the crops will die, now or later. She must keep getting food, or she and Loomis will not survive. She is very willing to do this – but is Loomis willing?

At the end of the diary entry, which has covered six days, and spanned three chapters, Ann is planning how to survive in the cave.

The chapter itself completes the account of how Ann has come to live in the cave, and introduces us to the fact that her new life, living rough, is not going to be easy.

It is also the beginning of the open battle between Ann and Loomis. What do you think each of them thinks about the battle? Answer these questions:

1 Which of these does NOT reflect the way Ann feels?
   a. determined not to give in to Loomis
   b. determined to get even with Loomis
   c. willing to work to keep the two of them alive
   d. wanting to live in the valley as friends with Loomis
2 Which of these do you think reflects the way Loomis feels?
   a. beginning to see that he may have to compromise with Ann
   b. still determined to get Ann to do what he wants

c. now only concerned with his own survival

d. wanting to keep Faro with him for company

Faro here begins to be more important to the plot than before. When Loomis ties him up, he suddenly becomes a vital weapon in the battle. If you have read the whole book you may remember why. In this chapter, in fact, Ann admits that she has made a mistake in how she treats Faro. What is this mistake – and why does it lead to trouble in the end?

Chapter 20

July 1st

Ann realizes now that Loomis has tied Faro up so that he can use the dog to track her. Late in the afternoon of 30 June, he led him out on a leash and, although they did not get far because Loomis was still weak, it was enough to frighten Ann.

Ann takes stock of what she has. She has to learn to survive on her own. What is she going to do about these things?

Food
Clothing
Warmth
Shelter
Light
Drink

The next morning, she goes down to the house to face Loomis. They face each other for the first time since the attempted rape. What do you think Loomis is feeling at this time? Read carefully the account of their meeting, from p.142 through to p.144, when Loomis goes back into the house. Notice what he says and does, and what Ann imagines his feelings to be. Now write another account of the meeting, this time from Loomis's point of view. Be sure to have the characters saying the same words as they do in the original, but this time also include what Loomis sees, hears and feels.

Ann herself is even more suspicious of Loomis. She begins to realize, for the first time, that he plans to keep her a prisoner, once he has her back. She now knows what the end of the battle will be, unless she wins it.

Ann does her day's work, and at the end of the day, she returns to the cave, and there once again sees Loomis trying to track her. He also drives the tractor, to check that he can do so.

Ann ends the day by building and lighting her fire, checking that it cannot be seen from the house, and eating. She also has some significant thoughts about life outside the valley.

This chapter is another lull in the hostilities, a kind of truce between them. But whereas Ann does not want the fighting to start again, and does her best to work for and with Loomis, he is still only concerned with beating her.

This all leads to the beginning of Ann's change of heart. Up to now, she has always concentrated on making the life inside the valley work, even when things with Loomis have got difficult.

Read the final paragraphs of the chapter again, and then answer these questions about them.

1 What is Ann's attitude towards Loomis now?
2 What does she wish had happened to him when he came to the valley?
3 What does she realize, for the first time, about other valleys in the area?
4 What do you think Ann begins to think at this time that she has never thought before?

Chapter 21

August 4th

Ann is not sure of the exact date.

Again, Ann is writing weeks later of what has happened since she last wrote her diary.

The uneasy truce between her and Loomis lasts for about ten days. She does the work, leaving him food each day and taking some for herself. She misses many things about living in the house, but for the moment she is safe.

She sees Loomis from a distance, taking the tractor out, tracking with Faro, and, one day, actually looking for Ann. She avoids him by approaching the farm a different way that day, so that he cannot see where she is coming from.

What happens next is vital to the book, for it enables Loomis to discover where Ann is hiding out. Read the section from p.152, where Ann begins work, to p.156, when she realizes her mistake, and then put these events in the order in which they happened.

1 Ann leaves the water can by the pond.
2 Ann and Loomis talk.
3 Ann eats her lunch.
4 Ann begins work.
5 Ann realizes she has left her milk pail and egg sack in the cave.
6 Ann realizes Loomis has the key to the tractor.
7 Ann realizes Loomis can now work out her hiding-place.
8 Loomis thanks Ann for bringing the knife back with her.
9 Ann brings the milk pail and knife back from the cave.
10 Ann realizes that Loomis has timed her journey to and from the pond.
11 Ann decides to go back to the cave.
12 Ann goes to the cave.

When Ann discovers that Loomis has kept the key to the tractor, this is her first warning that he is about to attack again. At first he is pleasant, but then he tells her that he may not allow her to have access to things. He is trying, by this, to put extra pressure on her – in fact, he is trying to blackmail her, to bring her to heel. His situation is much stronger now that he is physically stronger, and now that he knows roughly where she is living.

With no work to do, Ann returns to the cave, and then goes fishing.

In this chapter, the next climax of the book approaches. The lull before the storm is at an end, and Loomis is on the attack again.

Read these things that Loomis says. What do they show us about him?

'If you are going to continue this stupidity . . there are things you are going to have to do without.'

'Possibly I will fertilize the wheat myself.'
'. . . I suppose you should have [the stove], too, after you worked so
 hard to move it.'

Notice how Ann is still willing to believe the best of Loomis, and
always ready to admit when she herself is wrong, or stupid. Even
after what he has done, although she knows when he is lying or being
insincere, she does not like to admit how vicious he is.

 This chapter shows an escalation of the battle, and the next chapter
turns it into outright war.

Chapter 22

August 4th (continued)

Her fishing finished, Ann leaves a share for Loomis and then heads
home. She has gone only a short way when she hears Loomis following her on the tractor.

 What happens then? Pair off these sentences to form an account of
what happens and why.

Loomis drives the tractor . . .
He carries a rifle . . .
He goes to the store and looks around . . .
He finds nothing . . .
He realizes Ann has another place to live . . .
He puts locks on the doors . . .

. . . because he thinks Ann is living there.
. . . because Ann has left the place neat and tidy.
. . . to chase after Ann as quickly as possible.
. . . to protect himself against her.
. . . so she could not get back inside.
. . . because Ann has only visited the apartment once.

Once Ann realizes what Loomis has done, having checked the door
padlocks, she retreats to the cave again. She has realized that Loomis

is beginning to put her in a state of siege, with no access to anything any more.

This chapter continues to build up the tension to the point where Loomis shoots Ann. We continue to see him attack her, using first one way then another, in the hope of making her submit. We have no certain idea of what is going on in his mind, but you may be able to guess.

Ann meanwhile realizes that Loomis is not even going to keep the uneasy truce – he is determined to defeat her, even if it means starving her. She is beginning to understand the way Loomis's mind is working; what evidence do you have of that from this chapter? In finding out the way Loomis's mind is working, Ann gains valuable information that will help her survive later on.

This chapter also contains a little reference to life before Loomis, when Ann remembers visiting the Kleins' apartment. How do you think Ann felt when she went there, knowing they would never come back? Why do you think the author included that incident, at this point in the book?

Chapter 23

August 4th (continued)

The following morning, Ann wonders if she is panicking without reason, that perhaps the padlocks are not so serious as they seem. But she is still worried as she goes down to the house.

She decides to ask Loomis what he means by the padlocks, so she goes up to the house, and is just about to approach the front door when there is a sudden noise and a pain in her leg. As a rifle barrel appears behind the upstairs curtain, she realizes he is shooting at her, once, twice.

Ann runs for her life, to the trees beside the creek. She hides, to examine her ankle which the bullet has nicked. She realizes she has no way of caring for the wound, but she fetches soap from the cave and washes her ankle.

It is at that point that she realizes exactly what Loomis is planning;

to maim her, catch her and keep her in the house. She is petrified at the thought.

As she sits thinking, she hears the tractor; she runs for it, and sees Loomis drive out to the store, with his rifle, and Faro. With the dog, he starts to track Ann.

Loomis tracks her for an hour, Ann limping ahead to the cave to fetch a few things, then going higher up the hill to watch as Loomis and the dog come nearer and nearer.

It is at this point that Ann realizes that she has to kill Faro, to stop Loomis from finding her. Read the section on p.69 where she has a chance to do so, and doesn't. Why does she stop at the last moment?

What reasons do you think Robert O'Brien has for including this incident? Read this list of reasons, choose those which you agree with, then write a paragraph explaining your view; back up your view with examples if you can.

To show us more about Ann's character
To show us more about Loomis's character
To make us feel scared, then relieved
To show us the difference between Ann and Loomis
To show us how he, the author, feels about violence

When Ann fails to kill Faro, he leads Loomis to the cave. They stay there for a while, and Ann sees smoke; when they leave, and she returns to the cave, it is to find the place almost destroyed. Her things have been burnt or smashed, her fire wall broken down.

The diary entry for 4 August ends here; it has covered several weeks, since 1 July, and spanned three chapters.

Chapter 23 tells of the shooting. The fact that Loomis shoots Ann, when she has not threatened him in any way, is terrible. It is because Ann would not think of doing such a thing that she does not expect it, and walks straight into it.

Why do you think Loomis does this; is it, as Ann says, to keep her captive? What do you think is going through Loomis's mind as he prepares to shoot, then chases after her. Can you think of any reason to sympathize with what he does? Does Ann think of any reason?

At the end of the chapter, Ann comments that she is as bad as Loomis because, although she did not pull the trigger, she decided to kill Faro. Do you agree with her?

Chapter 24

August 6th

Two days later, in another diary entry, Ann remembers what happened after she was shot. She also says she has decided to leave the valley.

For several days after the shooting, she is ill, unable to move and in hiding. She guesses that Loomis has supposed she was not injured, so is not making any attempt to look for her.

Ann also describes a dream she has, that has remained with her. It is that she can live outside the valley, that there are other people alive in the world. She always wanted to be a teacher, and gave up that hope after the war; now she dreams that there are children waiting in a schoolroom for her to come and teach them.

She slowly realizes that her dream can be reality, if only she can put it into practice. She will need to take the cart and the suit, risking being killed by Loomis.

At present he is ignoring her; she watches sometimes from a distance, and he never notices her. And he never comes looking for her either. Why do you think this is?

How does Ann survive during this time? How does she provide these things for herself?

Food
Clothing
Warmth
Shelter
Light
Drink

What other problems do you think she has? What other strains are there on her? Make a list.

The situation cannot go on for ever; Loomis knows that Ann is desperate, so he sets a trap for her. She finds the store door open one afternoon; at first she is amazed and then excited at the thought of all the good things she might be able to take from inside. But as she is approaching the store, a rabbit runs out from under her feet, and as she leaps backwards, Loomis shoots at her again. It was all a trap.

She runs for the trees, and then watches as Loomis comes out of the store and begins to track her with Faro. She eventually hides behind a stone near the crossing of the contaminated Burden Creek, and watches as Loomis and Faro get nearer. She sights the gun as Faro reaches for the water, and as Loomis pulls him back, she aims above their heads and fires.

Loomis runs away, but Faro plunges into the water and swims across. He finds Ann, and she takes him to her camp and tries to feed him. But he is sick, and by evening the next day, he is dead.

The three important things about this chapter are Loomis's trap, Faro's death and Ann's plan to leave the valley.

Loomis's trap shows us that he is still determined to capture Ann. He has not changed, although when she shoots at him, he runs away. What does this tell us about Loomis? Can you imagine what he is feeling and thinking as he reaches the house again after Ann has fired the gun; what changes will this have made in the way he thinks?

Ann is at first taken in by the trap. She has survived bravely through tremendous hardship, and the temptation of the store is too much for her.

When Loomis follows her, she shoots at him, though she is careful to aim above his head; this shows how much she has changed since the time, all those chapters ago, when she welcomed Loomis into the valley.

It is in this chapter that Faro dies. You might like to ask yourself why it is important that he does die. What is the author saying to us, what message is he giving; what does it show us about the characters of Ann and Loomis; what effect is Faro's death meant to have on us, the readers?

Ann does not seem overwhelmed by Faro's death. It is almost as if she has suffered so much that she cannot feel sorry over it. But she does decide to leave the valley.

Why does Ann decide to do this? Make a list of all the reasons you can think of, and then write another diary entry, as if you were Ann, giving your reasons for leaving. Which of the reasons do you think show that Ann is growing up?

Chapter 25

August 7th

The following day, Ann writes her diary after she has stolen the safe-suit. She is waiting for a last meeting with Loomis, before she sets off out of the valley.

While she waits, she writes of what happened over the past day. She buries Faro, then lies awake putting the final touches to her plan to leave. She has memories of playing chess with her father, and of 'taking the offensive', moving into the attack. For the first time in the book, Ann is doing just that.

Ann gets up before dawn and gathers the things she wants to take with her. Then she fills the water bottle from the pond and hides everything near the top of Burden Hill.

What do you think Ann is feeling at this time? What might be her fears about leaving the valley and what are her fears about staying?

She leaves a note for Loomis, asking him to meet her to talk. She is, for the first time, lying, and tricking him, so that she can steal. Do you blame her for this? Has she changed since the start of the book?

As dawn breaks, Loomis finds the note; soon he comes out of the house again, leaves the gun on the porch and then walks to the meeting place. Ann is amazed that he has fallen for the trick. She runs to the wagon, checks that everything she needs is inside, and starts to pull it down the road. She is aware as she passes the house that she is leaving everything behind, her childhood, her life up to now.

Ann imagines what Loomis is doing now. What do you think he did when he reached the rock and discovered Ann was not there? Write a paragraph as if you were watching him, describing what he did as the time passed and he realized Ann was not going to come.

In spite of the fact that she is afraid of what Loomis will do if they meet again, Ann decides to wait for him to come, so that they may speak before she leaves. She is determined to face up to him. She has left all her things just outside the valley, and she is now waiting for Loomis.

The way in which Ann leaves the valley shows us a lot about her. Complete these sentences to explain what we learn.

Ann tricks Loomis into leaving the wagon unguarded, and we learn
   that she . . .
Ann steals the wagon and suit, which shows us that she . . .
Ann cries over Faro, which reveals that she . . .
Ann will not leave without seeing Loomis, and so we learn that
   she . . .
Ann is determined to leave the valley whatever happens, which shows
   that she . . .

Notice particularly the ways in which Ann has changed, and grown
up since the beginning of the book. She is a different person now, far
more of a mature woman than the girl who, in Chapter 1, was so
scared by the stranger.

   Also, Ann and Loomis seem to be more equal. Strangely, it is only
now that she has started to fight back that Ann seems to be Loomis's
equal, though we do not know yet whether he will accept her as
such.

   The novel moves towards its climax, and we do not know what will
happen. Ann expects that Loomis may try to kill her, and that she
may have to kill him. She waits for him to arrive, almost like a Wild
West hero before a duel, carrying her gun. We are left in suspense
until the final chapter.

Chapter 26

August 8th

Loomis is desperate and angry. He drives to the top of the hill very
fast, ignoring Ann's warning cry and shot, and leaps off the tractor.
As he approaches Ann, he fires, and she is immediately convinced
that she is going to die.

   Instead of running, Ann stands up and faces Loomis, which shows
us a great deal about her. When he shouts at her, she refuses his
demands, and then challenges him, telling him she knows he killed
Edward.

   Ann found out that Loomis killed Edward, and she was horrified;
but she tried to come to terms with it and was willing to try to forget

it, to make her relationship with Loomis work. The fact that she knew now stops Loomis in his tracks. He has to revise totally all he has thought about this girl. He also is brought face to face with his own actions. It disarms him completely.

Perhaps for the first time in the book since his illness, Loomis shows signs of emotion. What do you think he is feeling at this point? What is he thinking about Ann? How do his thoughts and feelings change?

At this point, Loomis actually begs Ann to stay. He is desperate not to be alone. Do you feel any sympathy for him here? Do you feel sorry for him?

Ann does not change her mind, however. She points out to Loomis, for the first time, what he has done. She stands up to him for the first time, challenging him to kill her if he wants to stop her. She does not give way to his pleas to stay.

Do you think Ann is wrong to ignore Loomis's pleas? Do you think she should stay with him?

Instead, she leaves Loomis with the valley, the food, the tractor. She is bitter about leaving, but she does it just the same.

What are Ann's last words to Loomis? Do you agree with her when she says they were childish words – what do you think she would have preferred them to be?

As she turns away from Loomis and the valley, Ann expects him to shoot her, but he does not. Instead, he calls after her, telling her where he saw signs of life. What does this show about Loomis? Do you feel any differently about him because of this? In the end, how do you judge him?

Ann walks on into the deadness. She walks all day and far into the night before sleeping. When she dreams it is not of the valley and the past, but of the children she is looking for, and the future. The last words of the book are 'I am hopeful.'

This final chapter provides the climax to the book. Ann leaves the valley, and heads out into the world. It is a sign she has grown up enough to live her own life, and make her own decisions. Do you think she makes the right decision in the end?

It is also a sign that she has triumphed over Loomis; despite the fact that she is a woman, physically weaker than he, and vulnerable, she has beaten him by her intelligence and her courage.

Now she goes out into the world of the nuclear devastation. She may or may not survive (do you think she does?), but at least she will find out what is happening out there.

Look back over the book. What have you learned about the people in it – Loomis, and his attitude to life, Ann and the way she changes and develops? What do you think the author has been trying to tell us throughout the book – about the disaster of nuclear war, the problems of wrong and right, the struggle between men and women, the challenges of growing up?

Do you feel the book has given you any insight into things around you? Despite the fact that Ann is living in a time and a place very different from the one you live in, do you see any similarities between her and you?

Are there any parts of the book you particularly like, or that work especially well for you? Are there any parts you would change? Would you include more characters, or write it in a different way?

And, as you read the last chapter, is there anything you would particularly alter about the ending? Does it satisfy you that Ann leaves Loomis to go off into the deadness? Would you prefer a different ending to this one?

Finally (and in the end this is the real test of a good book, that both shows the reader something and is enjoyable) would you bother to read *Z for Zachariah* again?

Characters

ANN

Ann Burden is the heroine of *Z for Zachariah*. We understand what happens completely through her eyes, and everything that does happen revolves around her. So it is particularly important that we understand her fully, the way she is, the way she interacts with other people, what messages she has for us about themes explored in the book.

We know very little about what Ann looks like. She herself tells us that her hair is short and light. We know that she is physically fit and strong from the way she works hard and lifts heavy things. We also realize, from the way Loomis reacts to her, that she is attractive. But because it is Ann herself who is writing the diary that makes up the novel, we get to see very little of her from the outside.

We know a little more about her background. She is the oldest child of a farming family, with a brother and an adopted brother. She has lived in the valley all her life, with parents who care for her, play chess with her and chaperone her at dances. She has been to the school a drive away from home, and she went to Sunday school regularly. In the normal course of events, she would have gone to college, become an English teacher, married someone of her own age, and probably settled down in a valley like her own, to teach in school and raise her children.

But something unexpected has happened in Ann's world. There has been a nuclear war, the surrounding country has been laid waste, and her family has been killed. She is completely alone.

The fact that she has survived this long tells us a lot about her. She is practical, capable and, although we sense that she has been through a good deal of grief, she has also coped remarkably well with the emotional problems of losing her family and with living alone. She has used her intelligence and what she knows of farming to work out for herself how to survive, and she has used her awareness and common sense, her knowledge of people gained through life and through books, to remain sane.

Write down ten words which you would use to describe Ann. If you are working in a group, check out with other people and change your list until you have the ten words you want. Then for each word, find one thing that Ann does and one thing that she says (find a quotation from the book) that are examples of this part of her character. You can use these examples in essays you write.

Has Ann any weaknesses? Perhaps the main one, at least at the start of the book, is a lack of confidence in herself. When Loomis arrives, we see her bowing to his judgement, blaming herself for his bad temper. She thinks of herself as unable to do things, even though she knows more about farming than Loomis, and copes admirably with the mechanics of the tractor and the stove. Apart from this, we see very little wrong with Ann, and you might like to ask yourself whether you think this is realistic. Would it have been better if she had had more faults or been less likeable?

It is around Ann that the main action of the book takes place, the struggle with Loomis and the lessons we learn from it. At first she is wary of him, a stranger coming into her valley. Then she begins to welcome him. She starts to look for all the advantages of having Loomis as a companion.

Does Ann have a realistic picture of a relationship with Loomis? She has romantic ideas of a spring wedding among the apple blossom, and she certainly has no experience of a relationship with a man. But there is plenty of evidence to suggest that she does know what marriage involves, and even has a clear idea of a successful marriage. Her parents have stayed together, brought up their own children and adopted another one. Ann's memories of them are all positive, and so she has a good model of how successful a marriage can be. Also, although she values her own independence, she equally has the skill to make a relationship work. She can work hard, she does her best to get on with Loomis, to share things with him. She realizes that one of the reasons for their marrying would not only be for their own good, but to carry on the human race. It seems that she has a very realistic approach to a relationship.

Suppose that Ann had written a diary extract about her hopes and dreams for her future with Loomis, about what she and he might be doing in five years time. Write the extract she might write.

But Ann's dreams are soon shattered. She and Loomis are very different, and it soon becomes obvious that a relationship between them would be very different from what she imagined. Take your list of ten things you know about Ann, and for each, compare it with what you know about Loomis. How many similarities are there? How many differences?

Ann eventually comes to terms with what Loomis is like. And their relationship soon begins to go wrong. Complete these sentences to build up a picture of how their relationship develops.

Ann begins by feeling . . . of Loomis.
She is scared when she thinks of . . .
When he bathes in the creek, she feels . . .
Ann goes down to look after Loomis, which shows . . .
She begins to dream of . . .
When the illness is serious, she . . .
When Loomis gets better, his attitude . . .
Soon, Ann becomes . . . of Loomis.
When he attempts to rape her, she . . .
She still hopes they will . . .
When he shoots at her, Ann . . .
Finally, Ann realizes . . .

We see there the gradual breakdown of Ann's relationship with Loomis. Certainly she had high hopes of the future. When then did the relationship fail? Do you think there was anything Ann could have done to prevent what happened, or was it all Loomis's fault?

When it becomes totally apparent that in order to stay with Loomis, Ann would have to agree to be his slave, she again shows her true character. Rather than submit to this, she demonstrates the courage she has always shown, and decides to leave the valley.

Does Ann have any choice? In her place, what would you have chosen? Write a paragraph on what your decision would have been.

Ann's struggle with Loomis is the vehicle for the messages that

Robert O'Brien wishes to pass on through the book. His views on the main issues of war, right and wrong, the relationship between men and women, and the process of growing up, are all reflected in Ann's battle and her eventual triumph. And so, to a large extent, we see all these things through Ann's eyes.

Her attitude to the war is in many ways understated. She almost cannot bear to think of it at the start of the book. She refers to radio broadcasts, to the loss of her family, to what she has heard about dead neighbours; but it is as if she does not want to think about it. And this is almost more effective than long, horrific descriptions of the devastation. When Ann nurses Loomis, she does it efficiently and practically, coping with vomit and sheet-changing in a capable fashion, merely commenting that she doesn't think she would make a nurse.

There are no frantic outbursts against the politicians, the issues that started the war. Politics is not Ann's concern, nor is it the author's. Both are far more concerned with survival. Both are totally horrified by what a nuclear war means, and equally determined to put their energy into living. When Ann leaves the valley at the end of the book to look for other survivors, she is proclaiming, with the author, her belief that life can go on.

She is also proclaiming her belief that even though she is a woman, she can survive alone. Throughout the book, Ann is the proof that although she is a girl, she is actually more effective and more powerful than Loomis is. It is Ann who runs the farm, tills the fields, feeds the animals. When Loomis is ill Ann single-handedly nurses him to recovery. Despite her misgivings, she masters mechanics enough to get the tractor and stove working.

Emotionally too she is stronger, welcoming Loomis and his problems, even coming to terms with the knowledge that he has killed, in order to allow a relationship between them to develop. When he turns on her, she refuses to give way or be dependent on him, fighting off his attempted rape and surviving alone in the countryside. This battle symbolizes the fight between the two genders, and in the end, Ann wins. She has the emotional strength to choose what is right for her, give up the farm and leave the valley rather than be a slave.

And knowing what is right for her is also something that Ann does well. Consistently through the book, she has an inner sense of what is right and wrong, from her first misgivings when Loomis approaches, to her belief that she is wrong to want to kill Faro. She turns to religion occasionally, for a sense of inner peace, and stands up to Loomis's criticism. She does change her ideas though by the end of the book.

By the end, Ann has joined Loomis in lying and stealing, tricking him with the note and stealing the wagon. She changes because it is the only way to survive, and Robert O'Brien seems to be saying, through Ann, that ideals are all very well, but if it is a case of life and death, then some things must be done. But not killing. Even at the end, when Ann believes Loomis will shoot her, she can kill neither him nor her dog.

So we see that by the end of the book, Ann has grown up. And what Robert O'Brien has to say about growing up is mainly about Ann. She matures into an adult by the hardships she goes through; she learns to survive, physically and emotionally, and she learns that everything is not black and white. She also learns to fight for herself and to make her own choices in life. This, the author seems to be saying, is what we should do.

What have you learned by reading about Ann? Using the following list as a starting-point, make notes on the things that her actions, thoughts and feelings have shown you that maybe you weren't aware of before.

About the difference between right and wrong
About the process of growing up
About knowing what is right for you
About coping with problems around you
About getting on with other people
About fighting for freedom
About the differences and problems between men and women

Are there any other things you learn from Ann that have been important for you?

We've certainly seen how the whole book is built around Ann – she is the central character, she does carry all the messages in the novel. But how do you react to her? Do you find her fascinating or boring? Does her practicality fill you with respect, or make you think she is a country bumpkin? Is her emotional maturity appealing, or do you feel she is too good to be true? In short, do you like Ann?

A final question you might also ask yourself is whether, faced with what she went through, you would yourself have coped? How would you react if you were the last person on earth – and then found out that you had a companion, for better or worse?

ANN'S FAMILY

We never actually meet Ann's family, but even so they are important to the book. Before we consider why, make sure you have a clear idea in your mind who Ann's family are. Read the first two chapters of the book, and as you do, make a list of the members of Ann's family. You should have five names, including Ann. What else do you learn about them by reading those first two chapters?

We don't learn much about what Ann's family looks like. We know very little about them as people. We only know that it was a farming family, who had lived in the valley for a long time (since the creek is called after them).

But we can guess quite a few things, from what Ann writes, and also from the kind of person she is. Read this list, and for each sentence, show what you learn about Ann's family.

1 David moved in with the Burdens when his father died.
2 Ann and her father played chess together when she was young.
3 The family went out to see if they could reach other people after the war.
4 Ann knows a lot about farming.
5 Ann and her brothers drove the tractor from the age of eight onwards.
6 Ann thinks of her family when she is under pressure.
7 Ann's parents took her to Sunday school every week.
8 When Ann was invited to a dance, her mother took her and stayed to watch.

By now, you should be building up a picture of Ann's family as a close, easy farming family who supported each other. How else do you picture them?

They have certainly made Ann the person she is – or at any rate was at the time of the war; self-sufficient, able to face most things alone. It is because of her parents' support that in the end, Ann is able to win her battle and break free of Loomis and of the valley.

It is also, we guess, because of what she learned from her parents about what a good relationship can be like that Ann refuses to be trapped by Loomis. She knows deep inside that something is very wrong about what he is and what he wants of her, and this knowledge must surely have come from her family and the relationship she saw her parents have. For the contrast between Loomis (who may be old enough to be Ann's father) and her parents is clear. Ann is a girl who expects support, expects to be praised, needs affection. She gives it, unemotionally but in a very practical way, and this must be because she has received it in the past. Loomis provides none of this, which shows us a lot about his character. When Ann helps him, he does not thank her. When he hears about her parents' death, he shows no sympathy. When she comes to him expecting praise, he does not give it. Ann's family, though absent, show us a lot about what the relationship between her and Loomis could be, whether as friends or lovers, and is not.

Perhaps the most important thing about Ann's family though, is the fact that they are not there. By the time the book opens, they have gone off into the 'deadness' and are doubtless dead. This affects the book in a number of ways.

At the start of the book, the fact that they have been killed immediately plunges us into the reality of nuclear war. We see the horror of what it has done to Ann by making her an orphan, and imagine what it has done to her parents.

But also, one of the main impacts of the book is that Ann is alone. She is only fifteen, but she has to cope alone – and does it well, farming, housekeeping and surviving physically and emotionally. This adds to the drama of the book, and in fact carries the main lesson – that Ann can survive on her own, and can eventually win through, purely by her own effort. At an age when many people are still dependent on their family, Ann has no choice but to live without hers.

FARO

Faro is the Burden family dog. In fact, he is not Ann's, but belongs to her 'adopted brother' David, who is now dead.

Some novels which have animals as characters, treat these animals as if they were people, with thoughts and feelings of their own. This is not the case in *Z for Zachariah*. Perhaps the fact that Ann comes from a farming family means that she treats animals in a very practical way. Perhaps, to keep the viewpoint of the story only with Ann, the author has avoided considering Faro too deeply.

At any rate, Faro has no clear character as such. We learn that he is a mongrel, mostly setter, and that he loves to hunt. This fact, that Faro is an enthusiastic hunting dog, is vital at the climax of the book, when Loomis uses him to hunt Ann.

Faro has a number of uses in the book, as part of the plot, to show us more about the characters of both Ann and Loomis, and also to stand for a number of things that Ann associates with her childhood.

At the start of the book, Faro returns to the valley having been to look for David. This in itself is important; at the time, Ann merely thinks that he must have survived outside the protected valley. As time goes on, she realizes that he is proof that her valley is not the only safe place to be – and this spurs her on, in the final chapters, to leave.

During the book itself, Faro is company for Ann, going with her to the fields, accompanying her to the chapel to pray for Loomis, and finding a young bird there. We feel that in some ways, Faro and Ann could have survived very well with just each other for company.

Also, when Loomis attacks Ann, it is Faro's growling that awakens her, and so saves her. He is the warning signal that allows her to fight back and so escape.

But in many ways, Faro is also a threat to Ann. She realizes when the stranger first enters the valley that Faro could lead him to her. But she forgets this, and when Loomis attacks, makes the fatal mistake of not keeping Faro with her, so allowing Loomis to use him for tracking. It is Faro who finds Ann's cave, and so allows Loomis to burn all her things.

Were you in Ann's place then, what would you have done? Consider these options that she had, and for each, think of at least one reason why she should have done so, and one reason why she shouldn't.

1 Crept down to the house, released Faro to run free.
2 Released Faro and kept him with her.
3 Shot him as soon as she had the chance.
4 Taken Faro to the deadness and let him loose.

In the end, when Ann shoots at Loomis, Faro falls into the water, and although in some ways, she is unemotional when the dog later dies, it is this that finally persuades her to leave the valley.

So in many ways, Faro is vital to the action of the book. He also shows us a great deal about the two main characters, and particularly in the contrast between them.

Loomis uses the dog for his own ends. He feeds it only to trap and tie it up, and afterwards uses the dog to hunt another human being.

It is Ann who befriends the dog, feeds it, keeps it as company. Although she treats the dog with the unemotional attitude of a country person, she nevertheless values it, and in the end, sheds tears as she leaves the valley remembering Faro.

When there seems no alternative but to shoot Faro, Ann's decision to do so shows us how she has changed, and how much under attack she must be in order to consider such a thing. When she eventually cannot bring herself to do it, we realize that she has retained some compassion after all, though she herself sees things differently.

Ann comments that 'in the end I did kill Faro, though not with the gun'. Do you agree with this statement? Do you think Ann is responsible for Faro's death, and if so, is she necessarily wrong in her involvement?

Does Faro's death make you feel any particular emotion? Do you think the author intends us to be affected by the death – or to regard it as part of a bigger tragedy?

Certainly Faro's death signals the end of a particular time of Ann's life. It is as if, with Faro gone, she has nothing to keep her in the valley or remind her of the child she used to be. She leaves, passing her childhood home and thinking of Faro, but seeing them as part of her old life, not her new life.

LOOMIS

Loomis seems to be the villain in the book. Where Ann is good, Loomis is bad; where Ann is strong, Loomis proves himself to be weak. He dominates her, nearly rapes her, drives her out of her own home. There seems to be no excuse for what he does.

We first see Loomis from a distance, through Ann's eyes, as we see everything. When he actually appears, we are already, because of Ann's fears, afraid of him.

His physical appearance Ann sees clearly, but we don't get a detailed description of him. What do we learn? How old is he, what length of hair has he got, what build is he?

We learn more about his background, spread throughout the conversations he and Ann have. Can you answer these questions about Loomis?

Where did he live when he was young?
Was he rich or poor?
What did he do in the summers when he was at school?
Where did he go to college?
What did he study?
What did he do after college?
Where was he a graduate student?
What did he research?
Who was his professor?
What job was he working on when the war came?

Having found out about his background, think about his character. At first, when Ann finds him, he is grateful to her, concerned that he is entering her house. She finds him worrying, though, and even before his illness he seems to assume he knows more than she does.

When Loomis is ill, the story of how he escaped from the city comes out. Ann discovers that he has actually killed a man in order to keep the suit. Edward, the other man, was threatening Loomis, and stealing the suit, and Loomis shot him. Ann thinks about this for a long while, and eventually decides that it is Loomis's motivation which is important, and that it is possible that he might have killed Edward for the right reasons – or for the wrong ones.

After his illness, he is truly impossible to live with. He watches

Ann's every move, he is fiercely independent, he is suspicious of her, he orders her about. Find examples of five things Loomis does that show you the bad side of his nature, other than the shooting and the attempted rape, and read them through carefully. What do they show you about his character?

Loomis seems to want to take over the farm from Ann and rule it completely. He is concerned about the way she is doing things, tells her off for not planting crops, wants to take control all the time. This is all symbolized when he begins to make sexual approaches to her.

It must certainly have been difficult for Loomis, not meeting any living person since the war, to accept living in the same house as an attractive girl without wanting to sleep with her. But he fails to realize that Ann needs a relationship in order to make love. She too has thought of their being together, but for her it is to marry and have children. What Loomis wants is instant pleasure, and to feel he has power over her.

Instead of a kind courtship, his attempts on her are aggressive, like the hand-holding, or threatening, as when he asks her to play to him. Eventually he can hold back no longer and tries to rape her.

Once she has fled, Loomis becomes desperate.

What do you think is in his mind during that period, when Ann is hiding in the woods and he is all alone? It certainly drives him to do some terrible things. While accepting her labour to keep the farm going, he tries to track her down, locks her out of her own house and stores, and finally shoots at her. In the end, he drives her out of the valley.

All in all, Loomis's actions can never be seen as right. He seems to epitomize evil, turning away not only from religion but also from the basic idea of being good to others in order to allow society to survive. As well as his more serious crimes, he also is very irritable with Ann, does not seem to give her the support she needs, and tries to play on her youth to dominate her.

In particular, Loomis tries to dominate Ann as a woman. He seems to have preconceived ideas of what women are capable of, and fits Ann into these ideas, ignoring the real Ann that he meets. So he is surprised that she can work so hard, expects her to look after him, patronizes her over mechanical things, dismisses her concerns, such as books, as unimportant. And he also assumes that her body is his to use as he wants to. When she does not submit to him, he attacks her again and again to make her his slave.

It seems then that there is nothing good to be said about Loomis. Yet things may not be as clearcut as this. Certainly he provides an enemy for Ann, which allows Robert O'Brien to convey certain ideas about Ann, and about the difference between right and wrong, and about the relationship between men and women. But Loomis may not be the cardboard-cut-out devil he first appears.

To begin with, we have to remember that whereas Ann has been sheltered from the effects of nuclear war, Loomis has seen the worst. We never know just what he has seen, or how this has affected him. Certainly he must have been under a lot of strain during his long walk to the valley.

In addition, we never do discover whether his murder of Edward was in self-defence, or whether he was acting with the wrong motives. He certainly feels guilty about it, and this may be making his life so miserable that he has abandoned all idea of right and wrong, and is just bent on survival. Ann, who has lived in the valley, has not known what it is to have to fight for survival. When she does find out, she too steals and lies in order to live. She does not kill, though.

A final point which may be worth considering is that Loomis seems a great deal worse, more irritable, more defensive, after his illness. To come through an illness like that may leave the patient damaged, in mind as well as body, and it could be that Loomis's suspicion and defensiveness are made worse by his illness.

What do you think? How much do you think we can excuse Loomis's actions because of the above things? Think about this for a while. Discuss it with other people who know the book. Then write about how far you think Loomis is responsible for his actions.

In the battle between Ann and Loomis that ends the book, Loomis is defeated. Ann takes his precious suit and the wagon, and leaves the valley. Read the final scene between them again, this time concentrating on what Loomis does and says.

How do you think he is feeling at this time? What effect does it have on him when he realizes that Ann knows, has always known, about his killing Edward? Do you think he really wants her to stay with him? Would he have been able to change the way he behaves if she had stayed? In the end, Loomis does not stop Ann from going – he even gives her advice as she leaves! What does that show you about what he is feeling?

Rewrite the final scene, from p.186 to p.188, as if Loomis were describing it. Have both characters say the same words and do the same things, but this time describe what Loomis is seeing, hearing and feeling. Does this help you to understand his character any better?

When Ann has gone, Loomis is left alone in the valley. How do you think he copes on his own? Do you think he settles down and farms, or does he become emotionally weaker and eventually give up altogether? More than this, does he come to realize that the way he treated Ann was wrong, and is he given another chance perhaps when other survivors find the valley?

One final important thing to consider about Loomis is what he is in the book for. There are many reasons for including a second character to counterbalance Ann. Choose from this list the five reasons that seem to you the most likely, then write five paragraphs, one about each of Loomis's functions in the book. Give examples, if you can, to prove your points.

1 Loomis is there to show us Ann's character.
2 He demonstrates the effects of the war.
3 He comes from outside to bring the war to the valley.
4 Loomis stands for what is wrong in people.
5 He provides an opponent for Ann.
6 Loomis forces Ann to grow up.
7 Loomis shows us what can happen when men oppress women.
8 Loomis provides excitement and tension in the story.

Finally, ask yourself if there is anything you like about Loomis; is he a totally unsympathetic character? If you were writing the book, would you write about him just as he is, make him more sympathetic or less? Would you change his character, or is he just right as he is, this last man on earth, this Zachariah?

Themes

RIGHT AND WRONG (GOOD AND BAD)

One of the main messages of *Z for Zachariah* is about the difference between right and wrong. It is not a clearcut message, that such and such an action is bad, and that doing so and so is good. It is far more complex than that.

At first, the whole issue seems very clear. We see things through Ann's eyes. She has no doubt at all that certain things are right and others are wrong. She also realizes that someone coming to the valley from the outside world may not be as 'good' as she is, will not necessarily share things, be kind, be friendly.

Make a list of the sort of things Ann may fear will come into the valley with the intruder. How many of them actually happen?

In order to understand Ann's ideas at this point, we need to look at the experiences she has had up to now. We get the impression that she has led a quiet life with her family and, though not ignorant of such things, has certainly never been the victim of attack or cruelty.

Also, she and her family seem to make time for church and Sunday school. Read through the sections in the book where Ann talks about church and God. What do you think her attitude is towards these things?

Ann makes no clear statement about what she considers right or wrong, good or bad, because these ideas are so set in her mind that she takes them for granted and does not write about them. From your impressions of her at the start of the book, divide this list into two, those that Ann probably thinks are bad actions, and those she thinks are good or neutral actions. Would she make different decisions under different circumstances?

1 Killing a man
2 Killing an animal
3 Stealing property
4 Wounding someone
5 Lying
6 Raping someone
7 Keeping someone prisoner
8 Being deliberately unkind to someone

When Loomis comes to the valley, Ann's opinions slowly undergo change. She is right to be wary of him, for his code of behaviour is very different from hers. Even at the beginning, he does not seem to see things the same as she does. She shares what she has, for she realizes it is the only way for them both to survive. He takes it because he wants to survive, but very soon starts to regard it as his.

Over the course of the book, we see more and more of Loomis's bad side. He soon starts to be unkind to Ann and dominate her. It does not take long for him to think of himself as the master of the land and her as the slave. When she refuses to do what he wants, he drives her out, and eventually refuses her admission to her own land. The word for this is stealing.

He has no time for religion, even when Ann's visits to church are an expression of her will for him to live. He does not understand her attitude, and his intolerance of other people's beliefs is one more proof that he is bad.

Also, while Ann regards sex, of which she has little or no experience, as something to be shared with someone to whom you are attracted, Loomis cannot hold back from taking what he wants. When he realizes that Ann is not attracted to him, but is afraid of him, he plays cat and mouse games with her, and eventually tries to rape her.

His ultimate goal is to be master of both Ann and the land. Ann has never tried to play power games with Loomis; she knows that is wrong. But his aim is to have her at his beck and call. So he attacks her, drives her out, hunts her like an animal, and eventually tries to maim her.

We also know that Loomis has killed, for Ann has discovered this during his illness. And when, at the end of the book, Loomis tries to stop Ann leaving the valley with the safe-suit, he nearly ends up killing her too.

Faced with Loomis, whose idea of behaviour seems so very different from her own, Ann does not know what to do. She tries very hard to justify his behaviour, blaming herself, sympathizing with him, sitting down and thinking things through. In particular, she comes to terms with Loomis's killing of Edward, and to see how she does this, you might like to read through again the section on pp.95–7.

Are there any ways that you can justify Loomis's behaviour? Read this list of things he does, then for each, write two sentences, one beginning 'I feel Loomis was wrong to do this because...', one beginning 'I can understand why Loomis did this because...'

1 Living in Ann's house
2 Scolding her for wasting resources
3 Taking charge of the farm
4 Attempting to rape Ann
5 Trying to force Ann to return
6 Tracking Ann
7 Shooting at Ann
8 Killing Edward

In the end, hounded by Loomis, and in danger of her life, Ann's ideas about right and wrong slowly begin to be modified. Again and again she offers him kindness, sharing food, working for him, hoping he will respond.

Finally, when he shoots her, something inside Ann changes. As he comes after her, she decides that the only way to protect herself is to shoot Faro. At the last moment, hearing Faro's excited bark, she relents; but afterwards is convinced that she has done wrong, just by deciding to pull the trigger. Do you agree with her?

From this point on, Ann acts as Loomis is doing, in order to survive. She lies to him by writing a note, tricks him into leaving the house, then steals the safe-suit and wagon. She has changed her idea of what is right and wrong in order to stay alive.

Go through this list of actions, the same ones as you read at the beginning of this section. Again, say whether, and in what situations, Ann now believes these actions to be right or wrong.

1 Killing a man
2 Killing an animal
3 Stealing property
4 Wounding someone
5 Raping someone
6 Keeping someone prisoner
7 Being deliberately unkind to someone

What changes do you notice?

What do you think of the way Ann's ideas have changed. Is she being more realistic, or is it sad that she is now willing to steal and lie?

Certainly Ann's change of heart means she is more able to stand up for herself, more able to get what she wants. As we see in the final scene, she is able to speak directly to Loomis, to challenge him and stick to her decision. Do you think the new Ann is better or worse than the old Ann?

At the end, too, Loomis seems less evil. When faced with the fact that Ann knew about his killing of Edward, and accepted it, he seems to break down. It makes us wonder if it was only his experiences in the war that made him like this, and if his actions have been all guilt and defensiveness. In the end he is lonely and helpless, and may be beginning to see that what he did was wrong.

In fact, when Ann is faced with the same choice as Loomis, she also chooses not to die or be kept prisoner. For Loomis, it would have been an underground prison, for Ann a valley, but it is all the same. The difference is that Ann, even at the end, is unable to kill.

But do you feel that, when she leaves the valley, she may well have to kill in order to survive. Do you think she will learn to?

And what will happen to Loomis? Will he change, or will he, without company, turn more in upon himself and become even more selfish and out for what he can get?

Finally, ask yourself what is your opinion of Loomis and Ann's actions. You have already considered how far you sympathize with Loomis. Do you think Ann did what was best? Should she have lied and stolen the safe-suit; should she have acted much earlier, and much more violently? What would you have done, if you had been Ann?

In some ways, the story is like another, much older story, that of the Garden of Eden. The valley Ann lives in is also a paradise, rich and fertile, untouched by the horror around it. Loomis seems to bring evil to it, by his need to dominate, whatever the cost. And like Adam and Eve, Ann learns the true meaning of evil, and leaves Paradise.

However by learning what evil is, she has also learned to defend herself and to survive. So, while in some ways it is sad that she has had to lose her innocence, at least Ann is now more equipped to survive in the world outside.

NUCLEAR WAR

The idea of using weapons that explode is not new. Gunpowder was in common use centuries ago, as we all remember on 5 November; its more sophisticated developments, the hand grenade and the air bomb have long been used as standard military weapons. But the concept of using explosives that could destroy a whole city, a whole continent or even Earth itself has been a real threat to mankind only over the last forty years. For almost the whole of that time, people have been supporting the stockpiling of such bombs, and other people have been protesting against it.

A nuclear bomb (there are many kinds, varying in size, use and effect) works not by simply setting light to explosive material, but by actually splitting the atoms that make up material, to cause an immense explosion. Tests were made throughout the Second World War (1939–45), but it was not until 1945 that nuclear power was used in warfare. The war itself was brought to an end when the Americans used a nuclear attack to destroy two towns in Japan – Hiroshima and Nagasaki.

The effect of these explosions was worse than anyone had anticipated. Not only were buildings and people blown to bits, but those at the centre of the explosion simply disintegrated – and those at the perimeter of the explosion, if anything, suffered worse. Even today, the effect of the nuclear attacks on these cities is being felt, by citizens still dying of diseases like cancer, induced by the radioactive dust that fell after the explosion. Nor was it only those present that suffered; deformed children were born to affected survivors.

All over the world, people were struck with horror at what had happened. Some were grateful that the Second World War had been brought to a close; and argued that it was all for the best. Others said the price was too high.

After the war, most of the major powers, and some of the smaller countries, decided that in order to protect themselves against being similarly attacked, they needed nuclear bombs of their own. Terrified that if this got out of hand whole countries would be destroyed, bands of people gathered together to protest at this: in England, the famous 'Ban the Bomb' marches, for example.

The situation is the same today. The nuclear arms are more sophisticated, and many countries have signed treaties promising not to use their weapons unless other countries strike first. In addition, nuclear power is being used with beneficial effects, in the fields of medicine and fuel provision, for example. However, many people recognize that as long as we have nuclear-powered weapons, nuclear attack could develop through human error or needless panic, and they call for all countries to give up their weapons and disarm.

The threat of nuclear war has, over the last forty years, hung over us all, and this has been reflected not only in the newspapers and television programmes, but also in writing, art and music. Many songs, plays and books deal with what would happen if there was such a war, and warn us against the horrors, or explore what would happen to people left alive in a world destroyed by nuclear attack.

Z for Zachariah is one of these books. Unlike many of them, it does not describe directly the terror of such a war. We only learn about what has happened through reports of people who have seen it. Ann, the heroine, has no direct experience of what has happened, and even at the end of the book, when she goes out into the 'deadness', we do not hear of anything very terrifying. In some ways, the nuclear catastrophe is only a backdrop for what happens between Ann and Loomis. Nevertheless, *Z for Zachariah* is a book about nuclear war, and its effects on people.

At the start of the book, tension is immediately created when we learn what has happened – that there has been a nuclear war and that Ann has, up to now, thought of herself as the only survivor. We learn nothing about why the war started. That is almost unimportant; it is as if the author were suggesting that anyone could start it, and that once the bombs were dropped, the reason wouldn't matter.

We then hear about Ann's first knowledge of what the war has done. Again, there are no gory details. We are left to imagine, from Ann's family's reactions, what they have seen. Why do you think the author has done this? Compare the way he has written the first chapters with the extract at the back of this book that describes in detail a bomb dropping. Which do you think is more effective?

Another way Ann hears of the war is over the radio. Again the description of the man on the radio 'pleading' is understated but horrifying.

Ann says very little about what she felt at that time, but you can probably imagine for yourself, and also think of how you would react faced with the same situation.

When Loomis arrives, he too brings some of the details of the war to the valley. He tells Ann of what happened outside, and how terrible it was. But it seems that what the author really wants us to think about is what the war did to Loomis, who survived, rather than to the people who died.

For certainly the fact of the war shows us a great deal about the characters in the book. Ann's parents go out to try and contact others, to help them. Ann herself, at the start of the book, has made no attempt to leave, but the fact of the war has forced her to survive alone. And this has changed her, made her self-sufficient, emotionally resilient; at fifteen years old, she has had to face the fact that she will probably be alone for the rest of her life, and that if she does not take care, she will starve to death. Her reaction to this, her practicality, her success in staying alive and sane, shows us a lot about her.

Loomis, however, has suffered. We suspect he is maybe a little mad after what has happened to him. In the beginning, in order to survive, he killed, and the fact haunts him, and makes him concerned only with his own survival. We wonder how he would have been if the war had not happened, whether he would have been a kind, relaxed scientist with a wife and family. We wonder too whether Ann would have been the same if she had suffered what Loomis did, if she had not been sheltered in the valley.

The valley does shelter Ann, but there is still no escape from the reality of the war. Loomis's arrival immediately plunges Ann into this reality – the safe-suit and the Geiger counter both remind her of the threat. Then Loomis falls ill, and over several chapters Ann and the reader watch as the horrors of radiation sickness take over. Does Ann think, as she watches Loomis suffering, that this is what her family went through – and when she leaves the valley, that this is what she herself will go through if the safe-suit fails?

At the end of the book, though, it does not seem as if these things are important to Ann when she considers whether to leave. What do you think the author is saying here, by letting Ann's desire for freedom outweigh her fear?

For in the end, although this book is about other things – the struggle between Ann and Loomis, and Ann's development as a woman – it is also about the fact that Ann braves the 'deadness' and goes back out into the world. It is also about a world where nuclear attack has happened, and the effects of nuclear attack on the survivors.

What is the message that Robert O'Brien is giving us about nuclear war? Do you think he is anti-nuclear, or has he just set his novel in the aftermath of an attack because it provides a neat way of isolating his main characters? What do you think?

And how do you feel, having read the book, about the problems of nuclear power? Does *Z for Zachariah* leave you feeling strongly against nuclear war, or merely indifferent? Would you demonstrate against the use of nuclear weapons – or just enjoy the benefits that nuclear power gives us today?

MAN VERSUS WOMAN

It is no coincidence that in *Z for Zachariah* the main characters are one man and one woman. It is also no coincidence that, in the end, it is the woman who gains control and, making her own decision, has the courage to go her own way.

Even up to fifty years ago, attitudes to the roles of men and women were generally the same throughout the Western world. Each gender accepted that, in order to make the world go round, and family life work on a day-to-day basis, men and women fitted into defined roles and stayed that way.

A family was usually a complete unit, with the man working outside the home and the woman working inside it, keeping house and bearing children (which only she could do). This division of labour, and the fact that it made the woman dependent on the man, set up certain patterns of behaviour in society. The man is usually physically stronger than the woman, and it was often accepted that he was more intelligent as well, having seen more of the world. In sexual matters, he often took the initiative, and he made the choice of partner in marriage. And from these clearly defined roles, certain ways of behaving were also expected; that the man would cope better emotionally, would be better at decision-making, would in general be dominant; the woman, on the other hand, would be less able to cope emotionally, would defer to her partner's decisions, would be more submissive. There were always exceptions to this, of course, but it was certainly a general trend, and because people had a definite role to fit into, the situation often worked well. Don't be misled into thinking that women were always unhappy with this state of affairs, or that it meant that all men were callous and unloving.

In this century, women have been able to earn enough money to survive alone, and have also had more control over when they would have children. The set roles of dependent woman and working man have broken down – and so have many of the expectations we have had about the way men and women behave. Look at and fill in this chart, showing how things have changed. Are there things that haven't changed?

THEN	NOW
Man worked outside house	
Woman worked inside house	
Man provided money	
Woman bore children	
Woman dependent on man	
Man physically stronger	
Man seen as more intelligent	
Man takes sexual initiative	
Man chooses partner	
Man emotionally stronger	
Man makes decisions	
Man dominant, woman gives in	

This change of situation has caused problems, and in *Z for Zachariah*, Robert O'Brien shows us how, in this day and age, people's attitudes to the roles men and women should play can be at odds. In particular, he shows us how a man can attempt to dominate a woman, and how a woman can fight back and escape.

At the start of the book, it takes quite a while for us to be aware of who is writing, and what gender he or she is. This is deliberate – why do you think the author does it?

When we discover that the writer is a girl of fifteen, we are immediately struck by how well she is coping, keeping the farm going, surviving the winter, now facing the threat of an intruder practically and cautiously. Throughout the book, in fact, Ann is presented as a practical, capable person who knows (better than Loomis) what to do and how to survive. She has learned how to farm from her parents, and she is intelligent enough to fill in the gaps for herself.

There are things Ann can't do, either because she is not strong enough – although she usually finds a way round this – or because she does not think she can. But not thinking she can do something is usually because Ann is not confident of herself as a young person, rather than because she thinks of herself as a woman. She never once makes the excuse that she can't do something because she is only a girl.

In other ways, though, she is aware of herself as a woman. Once she knows someone is coming to the valley, she wants to make herself look as attractive as possible. Very early on, she dreams of marrying Loomis and having a family. She is also aware of the dangers. She knows from the very beginning that, if the intruder is a man, she may be in trouble because he might be stronger than she. What does she fear might happen? Read over the first few chapters and see if you can tell.

When Loomis arrives, Ann is at first really happy. She has companionship, and she starts to plan for the future that only a man and woman together can create. And if Loomis had had the same attitudes as Ann, this might have been possible. But because Loomis is the way he is – either naturally or because of what he has been through – this does not happen.

What are Loomis's attitudes? Complete these sentences with thoughts of your own, then use what you have found out to write a paragraph about Loomis's attitudes to women and the whole issue of male–female relationships.

Loomis thinks that women are physically *weaker than men*
He considers Ann to be mentally . . .
He regards the fact that he is a man as meaning . . .
Ann, as a girl, makes Loomis feel . . .
He feels attracted to her physically . . .
When she shows her distaste for him he . . .
He wants Ann to come back to the house because . . .
He plans their life together as being . . .

As you can see, Loomis's attitude is very different from Ann's. He never treats her as an equal, always pointing out where she has gone wrong. He accepts her care of him when he is ill as his right, and never even thanks her for it. Eventually, as she realizes, though slowly, he wants her just to be his slave, and is willing to trick, attack and maim her to get what he wants.

The whole issue comes to a head over Loomis's attempted rape of Ann. We know that Ann has little sexual experience, probably none, having only had one 'real' date. Nevertheless, she is certainly, at sixteen, sexually mature and, having been raised on a farm, obviously knows about these things.

She definitely does find Loomis attractive, describing him as 'poetic' and noticing when he shaves. And she dreams of marrying him romantically, one day in spring. But Ann is certain that this will not happen for a while, that it will be when she is ready – and that they will be married, not just sleep together.

For Loomis, the issue is different. From the first day when he rests his hand on her shoulder, he finds her attractive, and is determined to get what he wants. His attempts at 'courtship' take no account of Ann – he talks to her a little, plays cat and mouse games with her, and then when she appears frightened, simply attempts to rape her.

Ann knows from early on that Loomis's attitude is wrong; she describes it as possessive, 'taking charge', and she wants none of it. If Loomis had regarded Ann as a real person, with needs of her own, rather than an object to be used as he needed, he would probably, in the future, have got all he wanted from her. As it is, his attempted rape is a failure. Ann fights back and escapes.

From here on in the book, it is a fight. Ann knows Loomis wants to enslave her, and he uses all the weapons he has in order to do so. What sort of life do you imagine Ann would have if he had ever caught her?

Every time, Ann proves not only that she can fight back, but that in fact she is superior to Loomis. What qualities does she show on each of these occasions that prove she is a match for him?

1 When he tries to rape her
2 When he tries to persuade her to return
3 When he locks everything away from her
4 When he shoots her
5 When he forces her to live rough

Realizing it is a fight, Ann has to change in order to survive. She already has most of the resources she needs. What more does she gain and learn that helps her to cope with what is happening and make her an effective woman?

One thing Ann doesn't do, which Loomis does, is to generalize about things. He has assumed, because she is a girl, that she is a certain kind of person. Ann always realizes that it is Loomis who is at fault, and that this does not mean that all men are like that. In the end, she goes out into the world, hopeful that she will meet other people who will treat her properly.

So we move to the climax of the book, where Ann leaves. She and Loomis face each other as equals, which they now are. It is Loomis who breaks down, who threatens, who pleads. Strangely, at this point we begin to feel sorry for him. It is now Ann who takes the initiative, seems physically and emotionally strong, makes her decision and sticks to it, and strides off into the outside world to live her own life. The roles are reversed, and Ann is a grown woman.

The story of Ann is not only a story about one girl. It has something to tell us about the role of women (or any group that is expected to behave in a certain way, and is dominated by another group). Read this list of statements, and decide which you think is nearest to what the author is trying to say. Then write a paragraph on whether, in your experience, he is right.

1 Men always oppress women and try to dominate them.
2 Women always are superior to men.

3 Sometimes men oppress women, and sometimes women fight back.
4 Some men think of women as inferior to them, and some women prove them wrong.
5 Some men oppress women; women should fight back.
6 Men and women are the same as each other – but if one group dominates, the other should fight back.

Finally, you might like to consider what might have happened had Loomis thought of Ann as an equal. There would certainly have been no dramatic story – but they might have had a working relationship. What would have had to change for Loomis, and for Ann, in order to allow this to happen?

GROWING UP

Z for Zachariah is certainly about 'growing up', in all its various forms. What do we mean by growing up, and why is it important to make it one of the main ideas in a book like this one?

Most cultures and societies accept that there is a difference between a child and an adult. Fill in the gaps in this chart to show the differences. There are no right answers – use your own ideas, and add on a few more categories, and then compare them with a friend's when you've finished.

CHILD	ADULT
smaller	bigger
weaker	
	older
sexually immature	
	more educated
less intelligent	
	confident
	knows when s/he's right
cannot survive alone	
dependent on others	

The change from child to adult is so important that many societies mark it with a ceremony or celebration. In some cultures, young people attend a ceremony – in the Jewish faith it is called *bar* (or *bat*) *mitzvah* – to show they are now adult members of the community. Many primitive cultures have long, arduous initiation ceremonies. In Western culture, 'coming-of-age' parties are often held. These are all to show how important it is that children make the change to becoming an adult.

One way to move along the road to becoming adult is to watch other people growing up. So both in real life and in books or plays, it is interesting to learn how other people have made the change.

In *Z for Zachariah*, we are offered a number of situations and characters that make us think about what it means to be an adult. Some are offered as good models, that we can learn from. Others are offered as ones to be avoided.

Shadowy figures in the background, Ann's parents are nevertheless good models. They obviously care for each other, encourage their children to be self-reliant, and are brave enough to set out into the 'deadness' when the war is finished.

Ann on the other hand, when the book opens, has stayed where she is. She is still in the valley, which becomes a symbol of the fact that she is still a child, not ready to face the big wide world, not ready to leave the nest. Which of the 'child' words in the chart above would you say apply to Ann when we first meet her?

In many ways, though, Ann is already nearly grown up when the book opens. She has survived alone for many months, and she has the knowledge and experience of farming to allow her to survive. She is nearly a grown woman, almost certainly sexually mature, and nearly at the age when she could legally marry.

But she still has some growing up to do. And the experiences she goes through make her do this. Complete the following sentences to find out how the events in the book mature Ann.

1 Her family leaving . . .
2 Having to fend for herself . . .
3 Being alone . . .
4 Coping with an intruder . . .
5 Nursing Loomis . .

6 Discovering Loomis's secret . . .
7 The attempted rape . . .
8 Being shot . . .
9 Living rough . . .
10 Faro's death . . .

One way of looking at it is that Ann needs to change in two major ways. She needs to accept other people for what they are, and she also needs to stand up for her own right to be what she is.

At the start of the book, Ann doesn't seem able to do either of these things. She is quite critical of Loomis, and she is always apologizing for herself, saying that she thinks things were her fault. Look through the book, and find some examples of both these things.

As time goes by, first Ann comes to terms with other people, then with herself. Caring for Loomis while he is ill, really hoping he will live, is the first step. When she discovers he has killed someone, her beliefs in what is right and wrong are shattered. But she comes through this to accept Loomis, and had he accepted her, would have been able to make a life with him regardless.

But he does not – and in the fight to be free, Ann grows up even further. She learns to recognize what is right for her, not to be someone's slave, and in the end is taking her own decisions. She stops apologizing to Loomis, and starts standing up to him. She stops believing that everything that happens is her fault and starts realizing that she is right and Loomis is wrong. She starts considering him as an equal, and fighting him to win.

Read over to yourself the final chapters of the book. What evidence do you find that Ann is now going for what she wants, not for what she thinks she should want, or what someone else wants for her? Find three or four incidents which prove this to you; get quotations for extra proof. Then write a paragraph comparing the Ann of the beginning of the book with the Ann at the end.

Ann is supposed to be the child in the book, the youngster; Loomis is supposed to be the adult. Loomis is, in fact, an example of an adult who is still a child in many ways. He certainly has learned to survive, and to get what he wants, but he has not learned to accept other people for what they are, and to work with them.

He also does not realize that, in many ways, Ann is more grown-up than he is. For each item on the list below, find an example from the book to prove it.

1 Loomis overruling Ann's actions
2 Loomis telling Ann off
3 Loomis taking Ann for granted
4 Loomis being less emotionally strong than Ann

In each of these cases, Ann is actually more of an adult than Loomis, and he is the one who is acting childishly. He, the only adult really described in the book, is not a good model for Ann. She has to work out for herself what to do and follow her own conscience.

At the end of the book it is Ann who shows how mature she is. As Loomis rages and pleads with her, Ann sticks to her decision and finally tells Loomis what she thinks of him. She says that her last words are childish; do you agree with her? She now has a clear idea of what the word childish means, which she did not have at the start of the book.

Loomis does seem to gain some maturity in the end, as he accepts her going, and even gives her a word of advice. But he never seems as adult as Ann does.

We said earlier that staying in the valley was a sign that Ann was still a child. Certainly as she leaves, she talks of leaving her childhood behind her. And so, when she walks out of the valley, into the real world that has been touched by war, she is walking out into her adult life. It is significant that, in the course of the book, she has had her sixteenth birthday, and has reached the age commonly accepted in Western culture as the age when a woman can begin to bear children. It is of children she dreams as she sets out on her journey.

Think about the topic of growing up. Does the book help you understand it any more fully? Do the things that Ann goes through remind you of any of the things that you think helped you to grow up? What else could have been included in the book to make it a more effective statement about the topic?

Extracts

These extracts will give you different ways to think about the subjects covered in *Z for Zachariah*. One of them, *Elegy Written in a Country Churchyard*, is the poem Ann read to Loomis on p.95 of the book. The other is from a novel that also deals with nuclear war.

If you know of any other stories or poems about nuclear disaster, find and read them. Be aware of how other authors treat the subject, differently from the way Robert O'Brien does. One may create a different story, another may have a different message to put across. Yet another chooses to include different characters, or write in a very different style. Some are much more dramatic, others more matter-of-fact.

What have you read about other themes mentioned in the book – growing up, for example, or the problems of being a woman? What different viewpoints do they present?

If you were writing about any of these subjects, how would you write about them? Would you write a diary, a novel, a short story? Which characters would you include? What would be your story? Perhaps most important of all, what message would you want your readers to take away with them?

FROM *DOMAIN* BY JAMES HERBERT

Miriam stood transfixed.

What was happening? Why the panic? And that dreadful wailing noise of just a few minutes before. The sirens of World War Two. Oh no, it couldn't be happening again . . .

. . . A young couple collided with her, knocking her back against a window. The girl went down and her companion roughly jerked her to her feet, one hand pushing against Miriam's chest. He shouted something, but Miriam could not understand, for her heart was beating too loudly and her ears were filled with the cries of others. The young couple staggered away, trails of mascara on the girl's cheeks emphasizing the blood-drained whiteness of her face. Miriam watched them disappear into the crowd, her breathing coming in short, sharp gasps. She silently cried for her late husband: Arnold, tell me, tell me what's happening. There were no more wars, not here, not in England. Why are they so frightened? What were they running from?

The sirens had stopped. The screaming had not. Stepping away from the wall, Miriam looked towards the lush, green park. She had planned such a lovely, leisurely stroll through those grounds, a journey to the lake where Arnold had taken her so many years before. Had it been their first time of walking out? Such a silly woman; who used such an expression nowadays? Walking out? But it was such a nice term. So . . . so innocent! Had life been so innocent? Not with Arnold. God rest his devious soul. In other ways, a good man though. A generous man . . .

A push in the back almost sent her to her knees. No manners these days, no compassion for the elderly. No consideration. Worse. Rape the elderly, slash the baby, were the latest perversions. Such things!

The people were swarming down into the Underground station. Is that where I should be going? Would it be safe there? They seemed to think so. If only I knew what I should be safe from. Let them go; no sense in an old woman like me joining them. I'd be crushed and they wouldn't care. Tears began to form in her eyes. They wouldn't care about an old woman like me, Arnold. Not these people today, not these, these . . .

Something made her look at the sky. Her eyes were not too good, but was there something falling? An object, moving so fast; was that what they were afraid of?

She blinked because her tears had stung her pupils, and in the time it took for that movement, Miriam and the milling, petrified tourists and shoppers around her ceased to exist. Their clothes, their flesh, their blood and even their bones no longer were. Miriam had not even become ash. She had been vapourized to nothing.

(From *Domain* by James Herbert, New English Library, 1984.)

ELEGY WRITTEN IN A COUNTRY CHURCHYARD BY THOMAS GRAY

The curfew tolls the knell of parting day,
The lowing herd wind slowly o'er the lea,
The ploughman homeward plods his weary way,
And leaves the world to darkness and to me.

Now fades the glimmering landscape on the sight,
And all the air a solemn stillness holds,
Save where the beetle wheels his droning flight,
And drowsy tinklings lull the distant folds;

Save that from yonder ivy-mantled tower
The moping owl does to the moon complain
Of such as, wandering near her secret bower,
Molest her ancient solitary reign.

Beneath those rugged elms, that yew-tree's shade,
Where heaves the turf in many a mouldering heap,
Each in his narrow cell for ever laid,
The rude forefathers of the hamlet sleep.

The breezy call of incense-breathing morn,
The swallow twittering from the straw-built shed,
The cock's shrill clarion or the echoing horn,
No more shall rouse them from their lowly bed.

For them no more the blazing hearth shall burn,
Or busy housewife ply her evening care:
No children run to lisp their sire's return,
Or climb his knees the envied kiss to share.

Oft to the harvest did their sickle yield,
Their furrow oft the stubborn glebe has broke;
How jocund did they drive their team afield!
How bowed the woods beneath their sturdy stroke!

Let not Ambition mock their useful toil,
Their homely joys and destiny obscure;
Nor Grandeur hear, with a disdainful smile,
The short and simple annals of the poor.

The boast of heraldry, the pomp of power,
And all that beauty, all that wealth e'er gave,
Awaits alike the inevitable hour.
The paths of glory lead but to the grave.

Nor you, ye Proud, impute to these the fault,
If Memory o'er their tomb no trophies raise,
Where through the long-drawn aisle and fretted vault
The pealing anthem swells the note of praise.

Can storied urn or animated bust
Back to its mansion call the fleeting breath?
Can Honour's voice provoke the silent dust,
Or Flattery soothe the dull cold ear of Death?

Perhaps in this neglected spot is laid
Some heart once pregnant with celestial fire;
Hands that the rod of empire might have swayed,
Or waked to ecstasy the living lyre.

But Knowledge to their eyes her ample page
Rich with the spoils of time did ne'er unroll;
Chill Penury repressed their noble rage,
And froze the genial current of the soul.

Full many a gem of purest ray serene
The dark unfathomed caves of ocean bear:
Full many a flower is born to blush unseen,
And waste its sweetness on the desert air.

Some village-Hampden that with dauntless breast
The little tyrant of his fields withstood;
Some mute inglorious Milton here may rest,
Some Cromwell guiltless of his country's blood.

The applause of listening senates to command,
The threats of pain and ruin to despise,
To scatter plenty o'er a smiling land,
And read their history in a nation's eyes,

Their lot forbade: nor circumscribed alone
Their growing virtues, but their crimes confined;
Forbade to wade through slaughter to a throne,
And shut the gates of mercy on mankind,

The struggling pangs of conscious truth to hide,
To quench the blushes of ingenuous shame,
Or heap the shrine of Luxury and Pride
With incense kindled at the Muse's flame.

Far from the madding crowd's ignoble strife
Their sober wishes never learned to stray;
Along the cool sequestered way of life
They kept the noiseless tenor of their way.

Yet even these bones from insult to protect
Some frail memorial still erected nigh,
With uncouth rhymes and shapeless sculpture decked,
Implores the passing tribute of a sigh.

Their name, their years, spelt by the unlettered muse,
The place of fame and elegy supply:
And many a holy text around she strews,
That teach the rustic moralist to die.

For who to dumb Forgetfulness a prey,
This pleasing anxious being e'er resigned,
Left the warm precincts of the cheerful day,
Nor cast one longing lingering look behind?

On some fond breast the parting soul relies,
Some pious drops the closing eye requires;
Even from the tomb the voice of Nature cries,
Even in our ashes live their wonted fires.

For thee who, mindful of the unhonoured dead,
Dost in these lines their artless tales relate;
If chance, by lonely Contemplation led,
Some kindred spirit shall inquire thy fate,

Haply some hoary-headed swain may say,
'Oft have we seen him at the peep of dawn
Brushing with hasty steps the dews away
To meet the sun upon the upland lawn.

'There at the foot of yonder nodding beech
That wreathes its old fantastic roots so high,
His listless length at noontide would he stretch,
And pore upon the brook that babbles by.

'Hard by yon wood, now smiling as in scorn,
Muttering his wayward fancies he would rove,
Now drooping, woeful wan, like one forlorn,
Or crazed in care, or lost in hopeless love.

'One morn I missed him on the customed hill,
Along the heath and near his favourite tree;
Another came; nor yet beside the rill,
Nor up the lawn, nor at the wood was he;

'The next with dirges due in sad array
Slow through the church-way path we saw him borne.
Approach and read (for thou canst read) the lay,
Graved on the stone beneath yon aged thorn.'

THE EPITAPH
Here rests his head upon the lap of earth
A youth to Fortune and to Fame unknown.
Fair Science frowned not on his humble birth,
And Melancholy marked him for her own.

Large was his bounty and his soul sincere,
Heaven did a recompense as largely send:
He gave to Misery all he had, a tear,
He gained from Heaven ('twas all he wished) a friend.

No farther seek his merits to disclose,
Or draw his frailties from their dread abode,
(There they alike in trembling hope repose)
The bosom of his Father and his God.

Glossary

adjoin: join on to

almanack: specialized calendar

Amish: American religious group following simple life

anaemic: weak through shortage of red blood cells

anguish: pain

anthology: collection of writings

asphyxiation: suffocation

bearable: possible to put up with

buckle: bend and give way

carbine: short firearm

carburettor: device for mixing air with petrol vapour

civilized: cultivated, populated

composition: essay

comprehending: understanding

confined: restricted

confrontation: angry meeting

conscious: awake

conserve: keep

contagious: catching

controversial: leading to disagreement

cornmeal: flour made of corn

corrode: rust

cosmic: from outer space

coverall: overall

cranny: small crevice

cupola: dome

dehydrated: dried out

delirious: feverish and imagining things

delirium: fever in which you imagine things

dependable: reliable

dogwood: a type of flowering shrub

dominate: master

dysentery: serious diarrhoea

emphatic: certain

enclave: safe place surrounded by dangerous land

fescue: pasture grass

flush: drive out

forsythia: yellow flowering shrub

frail: weak

freeze on a point: stop with nose pointing in direction of game

frenzy: madness

friction: quarrel, disagreement

furtive: secretive

generator: source of power

germinate: start to grow
gnawing: chewing
grave: serious
grippe: influenza

harrow: farming implement for breaking up earth
hill-billies: simple country people
hominy: coarse ground maize mixed with water or milk
hummock: small hill

illusion: hallucination
inconsequential: unimportant
inexplicable: without explanation
innocently: without evil intentions
inspiration: brilliant idea
instinct: natural feeling
intent: concentrating on
interim: in between

latitude: position north or south of Equator
longitude: position east or west of Greenwich
lustrous: shiny

merge: join together
mirage: illusion
mollified: made sweet-tempered
momentous: really important
monotony: boredom

normalcy: usual state

offensive: attack
operate: work
overseer: foreman

penetrate: get through

pertaining to: to do with
pitcher: jug
porous: letting water through
possession: ownership
prime: inject petrol into
profanity: swearing, blasphemy
proper: itself

radiation: lethal rays and particles
radioactive: giving off the above
ravine: deep, narrow gorge
reflex: unconscious reaction
relative: compared to
respiration: breathing
resume: get back
rotate: change the crop grown

sapling: young tree
specific: particular
squash: marrow, pumpkin, etc.
station: place on duty

tackroom: room where harness is kept
tension: stress
tether: tie to fixed point

unfocused: not seen clearly
uninhabitable: not fit to live in

vicinity: neighbourhood
visible: able to be seen
vitally: crucially

waning: fading
wary: cautious
weaned: no longer drinking only milk
wince: flinch

FOR THE BEST IN PAPERBACKS, LOOK FOR THE

In every corner of the world, on every subject under the sun, Penguin represents quality and variety – the very best in publishing today.

For complete information about books available from Penguin – including Pelicans, Puffins, Peregrines and Penguin Classics – and how to order them, write to us at the appropriate address below. Please note that for copyright reasons the selection of books varies from country to country.

In the United Kingdom: For a complete list of books available from Penguin in the U.K., please write to *Dept E.P., Penguin Books Ltd, Harmondsworth, Middlesex, UB7 0DA*

In the United States: For a complete list of books available from Penguin in the U.S., please write to *Dept BA, Penguin, 299 Murray Hill Parkway, East Rutherford, New Jersey 07073*

In Canada: For a complete list of books available from Penguin in Canada, please write to *Penguin Books Canada Ltd, 2801 John Street, Markham, Ontario L3R 1B4*

In Australia: For a complete list of books available from Penguin in Australia, please write to the *Marketing Department, Penguin Books Australia Ltd, P.O. Box 257, Ringwood, Victoria 3134*

In New Zealand: For a complete list of books available from Penguin in New Zealand, please write to the *Marketing Department, Penguin Books (NZ) Ltd, Private Bag, Takapuna, Auckland 9*

In India: For a complete list of books available from Penguin, please write to *Penguin Overseas Ltd, 706 Eros Apartments, 56 Nehru Place, New Delhi, 110019*

In Holland: For a complete list of books available from Penguin in Holland, please write to *Penguin Books Nederland B.V., Postbus 195, NL–1380AD Weesp, Netherlands*

In Germany: For a complete list of books available from Penguin, please write to *Penguin Books Ltd, Friedrichstrasse 10 – 12, D–6000 Frankfurt Main 1, Federal Republic of Germany*

In Spain: For a complete list of books available from Penguin in Spain, please write to *Longman Penguin España, Calle San Nicolas 15, E–28013 Madrid, Spain*

John Aubrey	**Brief Lives**
Francis Bacon	**The Essays**
James Boswell	**The Life of Johnson**
Sir Thomas Browne	**The Major Works**
John Bunyan	**The Pilgrim's Progress**
Edmund Burke	**Reflections on the Revolution in France**
Thomas de Quincey	**Confessions of an English Opium Eater**
	Recollections of the Lakes and the Lake Poets
Daniel Defoe	**A Journal of the Plague Year**
	Moll Flanders
	Robinson Crusoe
	Roxana
	A Tour Through the Whole Island of Great Britain
Henry Fielding	**Jonathan Wild**
	Joseph Andrews
	The History of Tom Jones
Oliver Goldsmith	**The Vicar of Wakefield**
William Hazlitt	**Selected Writings**
Thomas Hobbes	**Leviathan**
Samuel Johnson/	**A Journey to the Western Islands of**
James Boswell	**Scotland/The Journal of a Tour to the Hebrides**
Charles Lamb	**Selected Prose**
Samuel Richardson	**Clarissa**
	Pamela
Adam Smith	**The Wealth of Nations**
Tobias Smollet	**Humphry Clinker**
Richard Steele and	Selections from the **Tatler** and the **Spectator**
Joseph Addison	
Laurence Sterne	**The Life and Opinions of Tristram Shandy, Gentleman**
	A Sentimental Journey Through France and Italy
Jonathan Swift	**Gulliver's Travels**
Dorothy and William Wordsworth	**Home at Grasmere**

PENGUIN CLASSICS

PENGUIN CLASSICS

FOR THE BEST IN PAPERBACKS, LOOK FOR THE

PLAYS IN PENGUIN

Edward Albee **Who's Afraid of Virginia Woolf?**

Alan Ayckbourn **The Norman Conquests**

Bertolt Brecht **Parables for the Theatre (The Good Woman of Setzuan/The Caucasian Chalk Circle)**

Anton Chekhov **Plays (The Cherry Orchard/The Three Sisters/Ivanov/The Seagull/Uncle Vanya)**

Michael Hastings **Tom and Viv**

Henrik Ibsen **Hedda Gabler/Pillars of Society/The Wild Duck**

Eugène Ionesco **Absurd Drama (Rhinoceros/The Chair/The Lesson)**

Ben Jonson **Three Comedies (Volpone/The Alchemist/Bartholomew Fair)**

D. H. Lawrence **Three Plays (The Collier's Friday Night/The Daughter-in-Law/The Widowing of Mrs Holroyd)**

Arthur Miller **Death of a Salesman**

John Mortimer **A Voyage Round My Father/What Shall We Tell Caroline?/The Dock Brief**

J. B. Priestley **Time and the Conways/I Have Been Here Before/An Inspector Calls/The Linden Tree**

Peter Shaffer **Amadeus**

Bernard Shaw **Plays Pleasant (Arms and the Man/Candida/The Man of Destiny/You Never Can Tell)**

Sophocles **Three Theban Plays (Oedipus the King/Antigone/Oedipus at Colonus)**

Arnold Wesker **The Wesker Trilogy (Chicken Soup with Barley/Roots/I'm Talking about Jerusalem)**

Oscar Wilde **Plays (Lady Windermere's Fan/A Woman of No Importance/An Ideal Husband/The Importance of Being Earnest/Salome)**

Thornton Wilder **Our Town/The Skin of Our Teeth/The Matchmaker**

Tennessee Williams **Sweet Bird of Youth/A Streetcar Named Desire/The Glass Menagerie**

FOR THE BEST IN PAPERBACKS, LOOK FOR THE

PENGUIN PASSNOTES

This comprehensive series, designed to help O-level and CSE students, includes:

SUBJECTS
Biology
Chemistry
Economics
English Language
French
Geography
Human Biology
Mathematics
Modern Mathematics
Modern World History
Narrative Poems
Physics

SHAKESPEARE
As You Like It
Henry IV, Part I
Henry V
Julius Caesar
Macbeth
The Merchant of Venice
A Midsummer Night's Dream
Romeo and Juliet
Twelfth Night

LITERATURE
Arms and the Man
Cider With Rosie
Great Expectations
Jane Eyre
Kes
Lord of the Flies
A Man for All Seasons
The Mayor of Casterbridge
My Family and Other Animals
Pride and Prejudice
The Prologue to The Canterbury
   Tales
Pygmalion
Saint Joan
She Stoops to Conquer
Silas Marner
To Kill a Mockingbird
War of the Worlds
The Woman in White
Wuthering Heights